INDIANS
IN
OVERALLS

by

JAIME de ANGULO

with an afterword by

GUI de ANGULO

City Lights Books
Hillside Press

Cover: Jack Folsom demonstrating bow & arrow.

Design: Patricia Fujii

Indians in Overalls first appeared in the Autumn 1950 issue of *The Hudson Review* and is reprinted here with permission of the editors.

The Achumawi tales are reprinted from *The Journal of American Folk-Lore*, vol. 44, April-June, 1931, no. 172.

Library of Congress Cataloging-in-Publication Data
Angulo, Jaime de.
    Indians in overalls / by Jaime de Angulo; afterword by Gui de Angulo.
        p.   cm.
    ISBN 0-87286-244-5
    1. Achumawi Indians — Social life and customs.   2. Achumawi
Indians — Legends.   3. Ethnologists — California — Biography.   4. Angulo,
Jaime de.   5. Angulo, Gui de.   I. Title.
E99.A15A64   1990
305.8'975 — dc20   89-77724
                                                                              CIP

City Lights Books are available to bookstores through our primary distributor: Subterranean Company, P.O. Box 10233, Eugene, OR 97440 (800) 274-7826. Our books are also available through library jobbers and regional distributors. For personal orders and catalogs, please write to City Lights Mail Order, 261 Columbus Avenue, San Francisco, CA 94133.

CITY LIGHTS BOOKS are edited by Lawrence Ferlinghetti and Nancy J. Peters and published at the City Lights Bookstore, 261 Columbus Avenue, San Francisco, CA 94133.

INDIANS
IN
OVERALLS

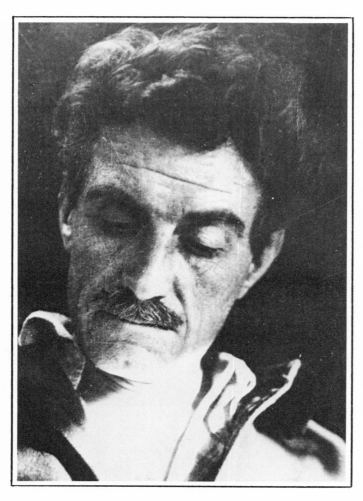

Jaime de Angulo, about 1927

1

A street in a little town on the high desert plateau of northeastern California. Clear air, blue sky, smell of sagebrush, smell of burning juniper wood. I was looking for Jack Folsom, an Indian of the Pit River tribe.

I saw some Paiutes loafing on a corner. I crossed over and asked them if Jack Folsom was in town. They did not answer me.

I strolled along with my hands in my pockets. Then I saw him, standing in front of a store. Same old Jack; squat, broad figure; very dark skin, gray hair; battered hat and brand-new overalls; and the same humorous, quizzical, gray eyes.

"Hallo, Jack."

"Why . . . Doc! Where you been all this time? What

you doing here now? Looking for another cattle ranch?"

"No. No more cattle ranches for me. I came back here to study the Indian language."

"What you mean, Doc? You mean you want to learn our talk, Pit River talk? You can't do that, Doc, no use you trying. No white man can learn our words. There ain't a white man in this whole country can talk Pit River. Some fellows, some cowboys think they do but all they know is a couple dirty words. Now, Modoc, or Paiute, that's easy talk. Why don't you try them? There is quite a few white men around here speak pretty good Paiute. I can talk Paiute, too. But Pit River, that's hard talk, Doc."

"Well, I can try, anyhow. Will you teach me?"

"Sure I will. Where you staying at, Doc?"

"Nowhere. I just got in on the train last night. Where are you living now, Jack?"

"Same old place. That little piece Indian land I got from the Government. I got a shack on it. Good water, I got a well. You been there before, Doc, you remember."

"Oh yes, I remember. Have you still got the same woman?"

"Yes, Lena. Big and fat. She still talks about you. She never knew a white man who was willing to sit down and eat with Indians!"

"Say, Jack, may I stay with you?"

"What you mean, Doc? You can't live with Indians!"

"Why not?"

"What would the white men say? They wouldn't allow you. They wouldn't talk to you. They would think you were a dog like us."

"To hell with the white men. I don't like them either. Will you let me stay with you?"

"Why sure I will! I have known you a long time, Doc.

But I ain't got blankets enough . . . unless you want to get in bed with Lena and me, but that woman is too big. Ain't hardly room for me alone."

"That's all right, Jack. I'll go and buy some blankets."

"All right, Doc. Throw them in my wagon. That's my wagon there. I'll go and buy some grub. . . ."

All afternoon we drove through the sagebrush. Strong and pungent smell. Jackrabbits. Sometimes a clump of juniper trees, rough bark, gnarled branches. Wide, wide valley almost like a sea. Barely notice the mountains. Canyons with perpendicular sides and rim-rocks frowning. Jog, jog, jogging team of horses, a bay and a roan, raising the dust. There jumps another jackrabbit. Afternoon changing into sunset. A turn of the road around a hill. A crazy fence. Open the gate and almost fall with it. "Indian gate!" laughs Jack. Another turn around the hill in the gathering dusk, and there is the shack. Big fat Lena comes to the door. She sees me. She smiles: "Hallo, Doc!" just as if she had known I was coming, just as if I had left only last week. That was Lena. Always took life like that, as it came.

I had bought a tent and I put it up in the moonlight. It was September and already there was a chill to the night. Jack brought a rabbit-skin blanket and spread it on my bed. "Bet you'll need it before morning, Doc. You don't see many of these any more. Indians too lazy now. Takes hundred and fifty, maybe two hundred rabbits. Well, good night."

I scooped a hollow in the ground for my hips and got in under the blankets. I smoked a cigarette and listened to the coyotes howling and yapping out there in the moon-light. After a while the pack moved away into the distance and their bark was very faintly heard. Silence and moon-

3

light through the tent door. I could not sleep. I smoked cigarette after cigarette. . . .

There was not much in that shack, except a few blankets on a pile of tule stalks in a corner. A good deal of the sky could be seen through the roof. There was a cooking stove, but it had no legs and reposed directly on the floor. Lena had removed the legs so that she could squat on the ground while cooking. She felt that was the proper way to cook, just like a campfire. Many Indian women are quite fat, but Lena was a very mountain of flesh, and getting to her feet was a strenuous operation. It surprised me to see how much she could do without raising her fundament from the floor. She could roll over and reach a frying pan six feet away. But "rolling over" does not describe adequately that peculiar motion, besides imparting to it something of the undignified. Have you ever observed in an aquarium an octopus creeping over a rock? It was a little like that. The rolls of flesh seemed to creep over the floor in advancing waves of cotton print, a brown arm uncoiled itself, the frying pan was reached inexorably.

Lena was not always cooking, although she always squatted on the floor. She also did beadwork, stringing beads of different colors in Indian designs, for belts, for hatbands, for tobacco pouches. The mind of a weaver must be a strange sort of mind, building a picture level after level. From side to side, from left to right, from right to left, it rises all along the line bit by bit. The whole composition has been visualized from the first and no retouching is possible. I used to wonder what went on in her head when her fat fingers got tired and she sat looking through the open door at the hills beyond. In the afternoons the sun came through the door, an autumn sun already, and the air was clear and bright. Lena spoke very little, and when she did it was in a very low voice, almost a whisper.

Big, placid, silent Lena, and her occasional chuckle. She and Jack got along very well. She was his fourth wife.

I said: "Jack, a while ago you called to me in English. You said 'let's eat.' Now, how would you say that in Indian?"

"*Laham.*"

I wrote it down in my notebook. Then I asked: "Which part in it means 'eat'?"

Jack looked at me with a very puzzled expression on his face. "I dunno what you mean, Doc, what part you eat. . . ."

"All right. . . . Never mind. . . . How do you say 'I eat'?"

"*Saama.*"

"And how do you say 'You eat'?"

"*Kaama.*"

"And how do you say 'He eats'?"

"*Yaama.*"

I thought to myself: Of course! That's what the grammarians call pronominal prefixes. The *s. . .*, *k. . .*, and *y. . .*, stand for the pronouns, I, you, he. I felt very proud of myself. I was getting along fine. "And now, Jack, how do you say 'We eat'?"

"How many of us eat, Doc?"

"What's that got to do with it? If I say 'we' I mean more than one. That's what we call singular and plural."

"I dunno what you call 'em things. I never went to school. But in Pit River talk it makes a lot of difference whether it's one man, or two people, or more than two people. For instance, you and me sit here, and here comes

5

another fellow, and he says: 'You fellows eat already?' Well, we answer in Indian: *Sahaama*. That means: 'Yes, we two eat already.' But if we had been more than two, like for instance you and me and Lena, then we would say: *Sahammiima*. 'Yes, we all eat already.' Just like you say to a fellow if you invite him to eat: *Tamma*. That means: 'You eat!' But if you are talking to two people you say: *Dzammi*. And if it's more than two you say: *Dzamma*. Savvy now, Doc?"

I was jubilant. "Why yes, Jack. It's what they call the dual. That's the way it is in Greek!" Jack had a very kind face, and it was now wreathed in smiles. He evidently felt very proud of the Greeks. He said: "Well, well. What do you think of that now! I always thought them Greeks were nice people."

I was astounded. "What do you know about the Greeks, Jack?"

"They was a couple of them had a restaurant here a while back. I used to listen to their talk but I couldn't get a word of it, although I know some Mexican too. I didn't know they talk like us."

Jack got up from the log where we had been sitting. "Let's go and hunt some rabbits, Doc." He went into the shack and came out again with his shotgun, and we wandered out into the tall sagebrush. "When I was a little boy I used to hunt them with bow and arrow. That's a long time ago, when I was a little boy. . . ." "How old are you, Jack?" "I dunno, Doc. Old-time Indians don't know their age. I'll tell you though, and mebbe you can figure it out. I remember I was a young man able to ride a horse at the time of the Modoc War. I was one of the first boys had the nerve to ride a horse. The old people were still afraid of them. That's why old man Folsom kind of adopted me. He was a white man. Him and his wife didn't have any children, and so they raised me like their own child. They were about the first white people to settle around here. When they died and I went back to my own people I felt like a stranger for a long time."

"Say, Doc, I want you to write a letter for me. It's to Jack Spring. You remember him, at Hot Spring, what we call Astaghiwa. . . . Well, tell him I got his colt ready. Tell him come and get him and don't let any them young Indians make him buck for fun because he'll be a spoilt horse before you know. . . . And tell him a Paiute boy shot old Blind Hall, you know, the old Indian doctor, over at Big Meadows last week on account old Hall poisoned his relations. He fired six shots point-blank but it didn't hurt him at all because he was not there. Old Hall laughed like hell about it. Said his medicine, Raven, warned him that Paiute boy was coming, so he went away and left his shadow there and the Paiute emptied his gun at it. . . . And tell him if he has got a rawhide to save it for me because I got an order for hackamores and quirts, and I am short of strings, and I'll pay him for it. . . . And tell him that old Bob Chief at Tulukupi is pretty sick and maybe he is going to die and we know who poisoned him, but we got some doctors on our side too. . . . Well, that's all I guess, and tell him take care of himself."

I wandered around in the sagebrush. I was thinking about this Pit River language. I could see already that it was going to be a very difficult language to study, a very complex language, structurally complex. And yet the Pit River Indians were accounted one of the most primitive tribes among the California Indians, extremely primitive, just about at the level of the Stone Age in culture. And so I wondered . . . Could it be that there was no relation between language and culture?

"I was born in an old-time Indian house, Doc. There ain't any more that kind left, old-time Indian houses. Nowadays Indian people live in houses like the white people. But that's no good because their houses are not well built like the houses of the white men. Indians' houses is nothing but shacks full of drafts and holes in the roof. Why! some of them is just made out of tin cans, you must have seen them by the railroad track in town, what they call Indiantown. This is awful cold country in winter, snow, blizzard, wind blows through. Indians catch cold and die. And we didn't wear clothes in them days and so everybody was tough and healthy. But now the Indians can't stand the cold weather any better than a white man, and even worse. We are all going to die. . . .

"The old-time Indian house, that's what we call *astsuy.* Now, I bet you can't say that word right, Doc." I tried and Jack laughed. "No, you didn't say 'house,' you said 'winter.' Them two words is pretty much alike, ain't they, *astsuy* and *astsuy.* One means 'house' and the other means 'winter' but the white people never can tell the difference."

"Where does the difference come in, Jack?"

"I dunno, Doc, I couldn't tell you, but they sound different to me. Any Indian will tell you they are different: *astsuy, astsuy.*"

I repeated after him again and again, and he laughed and laughed. Finally I caught on: it was a question of tone, pitch-tone: *astsūy* and *astsuy.* There are two tones in Pit River, high tone and low tone. Every syllable of every word is in either high or low tone, the difference being

Jack Folsom demonstrating bow and arrow hand position

about a musical fourth (as from *do* to *fa*). Of course the Indians themselves do not realize it any more than the average white man is aware of stress-accent in his own language. But it is an essential part of the Pit River grammar.

In the old days the Pit River Indians did not live in individual houses. In summertime they camped around in the hills and the valleys, here and there, moving about in small groups somewhat like our own families, fishing, hunting, gathering crops of roots and seeds, and practicing conscientiously a lot of good healthy loafing. In the fall, when the nights were getting sharp and the mule-deer were turning red, all these wandering small families returned home, converging from the hills, from the higher valleys and swales, down the canyons, through the juniper, through the forests of tall pine, down to the sagebrush flats, all trekking home to some wintering ground, at Astaghiwa where there is a spring of hot water, at Tapaslu where the valley ends in a cul-de-sac, at Dalmo'ma where there are lots of wild turnips, to all the wintering grounds, there to dig themselves in for the coming winter and snow and blizzards and days of calm with the sun shining bright and the air cracking with frost.

You can imagine them, straggling home, the men usually stark naked, or some with a loin-cloth or a G-string; the women wore a kind of apron or hula-skirt of reeds; they carried their burdens on their backs from tump-lines from the forehead or from above the breast, both men and women, for there was not much division of labor among these Indians, except that the men did all the hunting with bow and arrows; they all wore their hair long and often coiled it in a chignon and stuck a long wooden pin to hold it in place. There they come down the trail in single file, grunting under their packs, squat bodies with broad shoulders, skins of chocolate — although many are tall and lithe, like the Paiutes of the Nevada desert with whom they intermarried much. There are not many children because only the most sturdy and the most lucky can survive.

And now, from everywhere around they arrive at the winter grounds, one family today, another the next, and another, and another. Here's old Red Tracks and his people: that young woman there she is related to me, and who is that young fellow, seems to me I have seen him somewhere. I don't think he is a relation of mine, oh! and look at the woman of Stalks-in-the-reeds, she is packing a new baby. . . . *'Is kaadzi! Is kaakaadzi!* Man, you are living! Man, you are living! We got here five days ago. . . . Where is Standing-alone?" "Oh, he left us, said he was going to winter at Hanti'u, he has relations there. Has the old Blind Chief arrived?" "No, but there are four, five chiefs here already. . . ."

There would be forty, fifty, sixty people, wintering at one place, all of them, living together, living on top of each other, in one big communal house, a kind of underground cave. That was the _astsuy_, no, I mean the _astsūy_.

I should have given a great deal to be able to spend some time in one of those old-time winter houses, and see just exactly how did life go on, get a real feeling of their social organization, their family life, their kinship system. All these are just words. I had read them in books on anthropology, but they were just labels, dried specimens, lifeless.

I had always wanted to live with really primitive people,

11

real Stone Age men, and see how they thought, and felt. I had read books on primitive psychology, some of them excellent books like Lévy-Brühl's (who, by the way, never left Paris, or so I have been told), but I wasn't convinced. All that was too theoretical.

Really primitive people, not like the already cultured Indians of the Southwest with their sun-worship, their secret societies, their esoteric ceremonials. But real Stone Age men. . . . Well, these had been it, until a very short time ago. Here was Jack Folsom who was a little boy when the first white men arrived. Was there anything left? How much had they changed? My God, think of it, to pass in one lifetime from the stone axe to wireless telegraphy! Indians in overalls; no, there was nothing picturesque about these Indians, no feather headdresses or beaded moccasins, nothing to delight the tourists about these "digger Indians" in their battered hats and cheap calicos, picking the offal of the whites on the garbage dumps at the edge of town. My Indians in overalls! . . .

Jack said he had to go away for a while, had to go after a horse of his. He owned several good fast horses, which he raced sometimes, and made a little money that way. (The Indians had to live somehow or other — they had received a few pieces of land, here and there, from the Government, mostly rocky spots without water, useless — in the summer's haying time they could make a few bucks working for the white ranchers — the rest of the time, who in the hell cared? The sons-of-bitches were no good, liars and thieves, let them all die.) He said he would be back in a week or two. So, after he left with Lena and the spring-wagon, I saddled the remaining horse, tied my blankets behind the saddle, and went off for a jaunt.

I followed the Pit River downstream, stopped at Canby to buy a can of beans and some bacon at the store (Canby at that time consisted of one store, one blacksmith shop, and three other houses). The fellow there recognized me. "Say, ain't you Buckaroo Doc? Well, I'll be darned! Where've you been? Remember that time you rode to the show and you didn't have no pants on, nothing but a mackinaw and your chaps and spurs, and you walked onto the stage with a bottle of whiskey by mistake, and for a while everybody thought you were one of the actors? We still laugh about it around here. What are you doing now? I thought you had left and gone to the lower country . . ." etc., etc.

I went on down, and camped that night in a clump of junipers. Next day I came out of the hills into the Big Valley (*wa'wa atwam* of the Indians). I passed a little bit of a town called Bieber. Again I bought some grub at the store. The people there seemed to be half-witted and I had a hard time to make myself understood. All the whites in that part of the country are slow, uncouth pioneers. At least they were, at that time.

I went on. It was getting dark and I was looking for a place to camp. Then, not far from the road, I saw a fire burning and some people camping under a big tall pine. I went over, and that's how I made the acquaintance of Sukmit, alias Frank Martin, also known as Bieber Frank, also as "that crazy hunchback Indian doctor," who later became my inseparable companion — (how many ditches have we shared for a bed with a bottle of fire-water?!). Crazy as they come, long powerful arms, one eye gone, the other malicious, an enormous leering mouth with a few teeth here and there. He was a young man in his thirties.

"Hallo, can I camp here?"

"Sure! Why not? This is my land, Indian land, I am not like white man, I let everybody stay on me. Everybody welcome. I am Indian doctor. Where you come from? Where you going? Sit down here with us. I bet you never eat acorn-mush before. Taste better with salt. Old-time Indians didn't have salt. You eat salt and it give you sore eyes."

He turned to an old fat woman and started to talk fast in Pit River. They spoke much more clearly than Jack Folsom. Again I noticed the same curious singsong of high and low tones, of long and short syllables, like a Morse code. And what harsh gutturals! These two seemed to be always shouting at the top of their voices, like Spaniards (in fact, most Pit Rivers do). There was also another Indian woman sitting by the fire. She was little and scrawny, and she didn't say anything. Sukmit pointed to her and said: "He is my uncle. He don't speak white language. I ain't got hay for your horse. Will he stand staking?"

The acorn-mush tasted like pea-soup, more or less. There were also fried potatoes, but I had never eaten potatoes fried just like that, sort of parboiled in grease in a slow skillet. I found them revolting but ate them to be polite. Sukmit kept on talking and boasting. Once in a while, his mother, the fat woman, would stop poking the fire, look at him and say in English: "Oh, you are crazy." "She says I am crazy because I am a doctor, all Indian doctors are crazy." The other woman, the "uncle," did not say anything. She never did. She died two years later.

The old lady, however, I mean Sukmit's mother, was very active. Active, that is, with her mouth. Her backside never moved from the ground. From there she carried on a never-ending battle with her son. She stirred the mush while he went on ranting about his powers as a medicine-man, and every once in a while she would ejaculate the "Oh, you are crazy!" and there would be a short skirmish in shouted Pit River. She had a broad face, dark chocolate, and her eyes had already the thin veil of cataract. She was always gay and laughed a good deal.

Another woman appeared in the firelight. They said her name was Kate Gordon and she had married three husbands, all of them white men. "I like white men," she said, "they treat me fine. Give me plenty grub, lots clothes. . . . You want to marry me, white man?" I said no, I was already married. She was a handsome old girl, with gray hair and fiery eyes. She was evidently manic. (I have found that type, the manic, quite frequently among the Pit Rivers.)

There was something very friendly and warm about Sukmit, in spite of his shouting and boasting, something childlike. I had always thought of medicine-men as old and crafty. As I have said, Sukmit was in his thirties. He had a very keen sense of humor and was forever joking. But one felt a strange sadness, a wistfulness, underneath it all, and ofttimes he dropped into a reverie and went on with his work (for he was very active — always doing something, sawing wood, repairing his car, this, that) like an automaton.

I have seen other Indians, and many white men too, who often drop into this trancelike automatism. Fantasy is an active occupation of the mind which demands concentration, a narrowing of the consciousness to a focus. Some people can do it sitting down with their chin in their hand, but not your extrovert with his too much thyroid; hence that automaton-like activity — but the

15

mind is a million miles away. Sukmit had a drag-saw for cutting logs, operated by a small engine and a dry battery (at least he said it was; I don't know much about machinery and care less; like Sukmit's mother I was born before the days of the machine). The old lady felt a great admiration for her son, and a little distrust. I shared both attitudes.

Sukmit was a better informant than Jack, linguistically. By this time I had discovered that there were six modes in the Pit River verb: indicative, subjunctive, interrogative, volitional present or future, and optative (Oh, those so-simple languages of the primitive peoples!); but it was impossible to make Jack stick to one mode. In giving me a paradigm (I eat, you eat, he eats . . . etc.), he would jump from one mode to another. Not so with Sukmit; once started on one mode he followed it rigidly. The old lady was a different type again; she wasn't going to follow any paradigms. She changed from one verb to another if she thought it was more interesting — on the other hand, she was excellent at dissecting a long periphrastic form into its component parts. I would exclaim "Oh . . . I see . . ." and she would chuckle: "Ha . . . ha . . . ha . . . you white man!" When she chuckled, her belly also chuckled.

Sukmit and his mother were forever quarreling, usually in Pit River, but sometimes in English for my edification. At first it worried me but after a while I paid no more attention to it than to the breeze. The old lady had been born in an old-time Indian house. She described it to me in detail, and even made me a little model of it one day with sticks and bits of mud. She was very keen at explaining to me many apparently meaningless details, which become quite important when you consider the realities of life, and the necessities of a materially primitive culture. She had been born and reared in such a culture and had an artist's

16

Sukmit

eye for the significant differences. For instance she was explaining to me that there was no door in the communal winter house (which was really a sort of cave or cellar dug out of the ground and roofed over with sod) — people went in or out through the smoke-hole by climbing a stepladder set up against the center-post. But at one end of the house there was a tunnel that led out to the outside ground, like a rabbit warren. This was for purposes of ventilation, of establishing a draft of air into and through the crowded house and out through the smoke-hole. The chiefs, the important men, usually sat or lay there on their backs, smoking their stonepipes and enjoying the fresh air (forty or fifty humans including babies can make a thick atmosphere!). Now, mothers and fathers climbed the ladder with small children in their arms, or on the hip, or strapped to the cradle-board; but bigger youngsters crawled out through the rabbit warren; and the chiefs would grab them, and hug them, and tease them, as grownups do the world over. Such a description put the whole picture in focus for me. And again the old lady (who had a porno-graphic mind) would say: ". . . the smoke-hole pretty big — have to step across, grab pole — young girl take time step across show everything. . . . Ha, ha, ha! . . . you white man, ha, ha, ha! . . ."

The old lady Gordon, she of the gray hair and fiery eyes, was a very different type. As we were sitting by the campfire she told me of the wars they had with the Paiutes and the Modocs. It seems that the Indians liked to meet in two enemy lines facing each other and shoot with bow and arrow. Each woman stood behind her man, holding onto his belt, and passed the arrows to his hand. After the fight they danced to placate the shadows of the dead. They strung the ears on an arrow shaft and held them to the fire and chanted. Old Gordon took a stick and held it to the fire and chanted in a deep contralto. It was weird and made me shiver. For once, Sukmit was silent but old Mary had to break the silence and chuckle: ". . . Ha, ha, ha . . . you white man . . ."

I only stayed a few days with Sukmit and his people, that time. One morning he started to move camp, piling things into his decrepit automobile, and I saddled my horse. But his departure was in the grand manner. I must explain that Indians' cars, in those days, were of the "tin lizzie" type, held together with bale-wire. This was before the days of the self-starter — and cranking the engine was a back-breaking and discouraging task. Indians had discovered a very good way to start the engine: prop up the hind end of the car with a jack, then start the engine by spinning the rear wheels, then kick off the jack, run after the car as it zig-zagged through the sagebrush, climb in at the back, and grab the steering wheel. Very good, but hard for Sukmit the hunchback. That morning, there was a heated discussion between him and the old lady. He wanted her to sit at the wheel and steer the car while he started it Indian fashion. But she would have none of it. He argued and argued that it was easy, very easy. But she was obdurate. Finally he yelled: "Get in, Christ Almighty, do you want to live forever?"

I started back along the Pit River toward the Hot Springs. I saw a dilapidated shack and went in. There was an Indian girl in there. She was tattooing her wrist with an indelible pencil and a sewing needle. She sat in a chair by the window, pricking, pricking. She was tattooing two initials on her left wrist: B. H. Her face was fat, commonplace, and unreadable. She wore a yellow dress and her

19

Indian houses by the spring, 1989

legs popped out of tight laced high-heeled shoes. She sat by the window, pricking and mixing blood and indelible pencil into B. H. She was through the B and was starting on the H. Through the window one saw the flats of sagebrush and gnarled juniper trees, and in the distance Wadaqtsuudzi the big mountain where there is a lake on top and men go there who are seeking power. As I went out of the room I noticed an iron bedstead. It was held together by a pair of pink corsets laced from one post to the other. On a dressing-table a box of Jonteel face powder. I was thinking of that old woman who gave me wild turnips to eat at Sukmit's camp, she of the gray hair and burning eyes, who sang the chant for appeasing the dead enemies. She had the traditional tattoo lines on the chin. How she cursed the Modocs! They had killed her father and taken her mother captive. She also taught me a war-song, a monotonous kind of wail. She said her mother used to sing it when they were alone, and she would cry.

I had gone into that house looking for an old fellow named Blind Hall, or Johnny Hall (his name, I found out later, was Tahteumi, meaning "red trail," or "red track," or "sunset trail"). They had told me he was one of the most powerful medicine-men around. But the tattooing girl said he wasn't there; this was his house, but he had gone to another camp. She said he was sick. "He was going to town the other day with his old woman; they were driving along in their old buggy; automobile come from behind; upset buggy; old Hall didn't know he was hurt, but he must have dropped his shadow; he went on to Hantiyu, but he got pretty sick; he is coming back today; he is going to doctor himself tonight."

That sounded interesting. I thought I would hang around. Maybe I would learn something. So I wandered around. About noon Blind Hall arrived in the old rattling creaking swaying buggy with his old woman and the old old decrepit horse. I knew right away I had seen him before somewhere, sometime; that massive face, the sightless eyes, the very thick lips and quite a lot of white beard for an Indian. "Hallo, white man, I remember you, you stop once, we camp side road, you give me can beans, bacon, you eat with us, you treat me good, you all right, I remember you, I remember your voice — I am pretty sick now, dropped my shadow on the road, can't live without my shadow, maybe I die, dunno. . . . I doctor myself tonight. You stay, you help sing tonight."

Blind Hall called his medicine "my poison." The Indian word is *damaagome.* Some Indians translate it in English as "medicine," or "power," sometimes "dog" (in the sense of pet dog, or trained dog). Blind Hall was not boastful like Sukmit; he was full of quiet dignity; as to his age, goodness knows, he said he and Jack Folsom were young men together, and once they got mad at each other: "I called him by his name and he called me by my name" (you are not supposed to call an Indian by his personal name; that's too personal, too private; you call him by his term of relationship to you — uncle, grandfather, brother-in-law, or whatever — or by his nickname).

Blind Hall was groaning and bellyaching about the pain in his ribs. We were sitting in the sun. "Give me a cigarette, white man. Mebbe I die. I dunno. That autocar he knock my shadow out of me; shadow he stay on the road now can't find me; can't live without my shadow! . . . It's too bad, mebbe I die . . . tonight I doctor myself, I ask my poisons . . . I got several poisons . . . I got Raven, he live on top mountain Wadaqtsuudzi, he know everything, watch everything. . . . I got Bullsnake, he pretty good too. . . . I got Louise, Crablouse, live with people, much friends, tell me lots things. . . . I got Jim Lizard, he sit on rock all day, he pretty clever but not serious, he damn liar. . . . Sometime I doctor sick man, call my poisons come over my head, they fight, Raven he says that man poisoned, Bullsnake say no he not poisoned, he broke rule hunting. . . and then this here Jim Lizard he say, Oh! let's go home that man going to die anyhow!. . . Then Raven he shake his finger at him he say: Who ask you what you think? Why don't you help our father?" (The poisons call the medicine-man "my father," *ittu ai* — the medicine-man calls his poison *ittu damaagome* "my *damaagome*," or whatever you want to translate that word by: medicine, poison, power. . . .) "You can go home if you want to, we will stay here and help our father. Then Jim Lizard mebbe he stay and help and mebbe he tell me lie. I can't depend on him. . . . Ohh. . . it hurt me inside here. Maybe I die. Everybody die sometime. . . . I ask my poison tonight. You white man, you help, you sing too. More people sing more good. Sometime my poison very far away, not hear. Lots people sing, he hear better."

At this place of Astaghiwa (meaning "hot being," because there is a hot spring) there also lived Robert Spring (he took the name from the spring — but his brother was Jim Bailey, and why?? but Jim Bailey was the son of Blind Hall's woman, but Blind Hall was not his father. . . . Indian relationships are very complex and the adoption of white men's names does not simplify things). This Robert Spring was a very quiet individual, very shy, about thirty or thirty-five years old, well set up, spoke English fairly well. He asked me to show him how he could write his own language: "I been to school at Fort Bidwell; I can write English; I try write our language but can't do it. Yet you do it. Will you show me?" It was interesting to see that he was aware of the differences due to tones, but of course he had no idea of arranging tones in a sequence or scale. And *my* conception of a tone as "low" and another as "high" was extremely puzzling to him. "Why don't you say that one is to the right and the other to the left?" he asked. I had no answer, of course.

We were sitting on a log. He said: "Goddammit! an Indian camp is always dirty. . . . Look at that!" In truth it was pretty messy: broken wagon-wheels askew against a juniper trunk. A couple of shacks made of boards and flattened tin cans for roof. A tent. Piles of ashes, old campfires. Tin cans, tin cans, tin cans. A broken coffee-pot — but a beautiful panoramic view. Undulations of sagebrush and the distant mountains all around. This is a country of vast distances. That does not look like such a big hill over there . . . but it rises three thousand feet and it is about fifteen miles from here. Very fooling, this clear atmosphere.

A buggy rattled in. There were two old Indians in it, a man and a woman. "That's Hantiyu Bill. You wouldn't think so but that fellow is pretty old. He got that woman as a present. They used to do that in the old days sometimes. Her father and Bill were great friends and he gave the woman to him."

I asked him about that "shadow" that Blind Hall had lost. "That's what we call the *de'lamdzi*," he said. "Does that mean 'shadow,' like the shadow of a tree? Or does it mean shadow like what the white people call the 'soul'?" "I dunno about that last word, how you pronounce it? I have heard the white people talk about it but I don't

24

understand what it means. But the shadow from a tree, that's different. That's *dalilamdzi*. Yes, they sound very much the same, don't they? I never noticed that before, *de'lamdzi, dalilamdzi.* . . ."[1]

His mother, old Hall's woman, passes by. She is going to dig for roots, on the flats. Little old woman, all wrinkles, bent over under her conical pack-basket, tottering away with the help of her digging stick. She is eternally mumbling something. Once in a while she pokes into the ground, bends over, pulls a wild turnip and throws it over her shoulder into the pack-basket on her back. She looks very small in all that vastness of landscape. Robert Spring watches her and smiles: "See, she thinks she is helping. Old people are like that."

Robert Spring had a good ear; he would have been an excellent phonetician. He made me notice the difference between *dihoomi* "to run," and *dihommi* "the wind." A question of length: in one the vowel is long; in the other it is the consonant which is long. Quantity is as important in this language as it is in Latin prosody.

That evening we all gathered at sundown. Jack Steel, an Indian from Hantiyu who usually acted as Blind Hall's "interpreter," had arrived. He went out a little way into the sagebrush and called the poisons. "Raven, you, my poison. COME! (*qaq, mi', ittu damaagome, tunnoo*). . . . Bull-snake, my poison, come. . . . Crablouse, my poison, cooome. . . . You all, my poisons, COOOME!!" It was kind of weird, this man out in the sagebrush calling and

---

[1] I found out later that *de'lamdzi* is a noun, while *dalilamdzi* is a verb. Thus:
    salilamdzi — I make a shadow (on the ground)
    ittu dalilamdzi — my shadow (on the ground)
    ittu de'lamdzi — my shadow (in the sense of the soul)
Compare Latin *"anima,"* a current of air, wind, breath, vital principle.
The etymology of Anglo-Saxon "soul" is unknown.

Old Blind Hall and Jaime de Angulo

calling for the poisons, just like a farmer calling his cows home.

We all gathered around the fire; some were sitting on the ground, some were lying on their side. Blind Hall began singing one of his medicine-songs. Two or three who knew that song well joined him. Others hummed for a while before catching on. Robert Spring said to me: "Come on, sing. Don't be afraid. Everybody must help." At that time I had not yet learned to sing Indian fashion. The melody puzzled me. But I joined in, bashfully at first, then when I realized that nobody was paying any attention to me, with gusto.

Blind Hall had soon stopped singing, himself. He had dropped into a sort of brown study, or as if he were listening to something inside his belly. Suddenly he clapped his hands, the singing stopped abruptly. In the silence he shouted something which the "interpreter," Jack Steel, repeated. And before Jack Steel was through, Blind Hall was shouting again, which the interpreter also repeated, and so on, five or six times. It was not an exchange between Blind Hall and Jack Steel. Jack Steel was simply repeating word for word what Blind Hall was shouting. It was an exchange between Hall and his poison, Raven. First, Hall would shout a query which the interpreter repeated; then Hall would listen to what Raven (hovering unseen above our heads) was answering — and he would repeat that answer of Raven which he, Hall, had heard in his mind — and the interpreter would repeat the repetition. Then Hall emitted a sort of grunted "Aaaah . . .," and relapsed into a brown study. Everybody else, Jack Steel included, relaxed. Some lit cigarettes; others gossiped. A woman said to me: "You did pretty good; you help; that's good!" Robert Spring said: "Sure, everybody must help. Sometimes the poisons are far away. They don't hear. Everybody must sing together to wake them up."

The woman who had praised me for singing said for my benefit: "He ask his Raven if he going to die. Raven say he don't know; ask the others." Blind Hill started humming another medicine-song, and everything went on like before. That way four or five times. At one time he got pretty excited and started to jump and dance, and fell down. It must be hell to be blind.

The whole performance lasted about a couple of hours. Then everybody dispersed.

The next morning Blind Hall felt much better. I asked Robert Spring about the "interpreter." They call it *astu-mage*, which literally means translating or interpreting. According to Spring the medicine-man gets so excited that his speech often becomes quite unintelligible; but his interpreter is used to it and able to repeat it clearly. Quite so; he evidently performs that function. But I suspect something else, not so visible: the shaman is in a great state of excitement, it borders on hysteria, even catalepsy sometimes; it seems to me that it would be pretty easy for the shaman to slip into the autistic stage of schizo-phrenia . . . and never come back to reality! Is it not possible, perhaps, that the interpreter acts as a link, a life-line by which the shaman remains in contact with the reality of the material world?

Blind Hall was so pleased with my "helping" that he offered to make me some moccasins if I got him a piece of buckskin. Poor old blind fellow! *Some* moccasins!! They might have fitted the foot of a dinosaur, or some such beast, but not a human foot. However I assured him they fitted my feet like gloves and he was very proud.

It was Robert Spring who first made me understand about the *dinihowi*. "That's what we Indians call *luck*. A man has got to have luck, no matter for what, whether it's for gambling, or for hunting, for making love, for anything, unless he wants to be just a common Indian . . . like me."

We were lying flat on our backs under a juniper. After a silence he started again: "When a fellow is young, everybody is after him to go to the mountains and get himself a *dinihowi*. The old men say: 'You'll never amount to anything if you don't go and catch a *dinihowi*.' And then you hear other fellows brag about their luck at gambling, or how they got a good *dinihowi* for hunting. Well, there come a time when a young fellow starts to feel uneasy, kind of sad, kind of worried, that's just about the time he's getting to be a man grown up. Then he start to 'wander,' that's what we call it, wandering. They say: Leave him alone, he is wandering. That's the time you go to the hills, you don't come home, you stay out all night, you get scared, you cry; two, three days you go hungry. Sometime your people get worried, come after you, but you throw rocks at them: Go away, I don't want you, leave me alone. You get pretty hungry, you get dizzy, you are afraid of grizzly bears. Maybe you fall asleep and someone come wake you up, maybe a wolf, push your head with his foot, maybe bluejay peck at your face, maybe little fly get in your ear, he say: Hey! Wake up! What you doing here? Your people worrying about you! You better go home! I seen you wandering here, crying, hungry, I pity you, I like you. I help you. Listen, this is my song. Remember that song. When you want me, you come here and sing my song. I'll hear you. I'll come. . . ."

I said to Robert Spring: "But then, I don't see what is the difference between the *dinihowi* and the *damaa-*

29

gome . . . . " "There is no difference. It's all the same. Only the *damaagome* that's for doctors." "How does the doctor get his *damaagomes*?" "Just like you and me get a *dinihowi*. He goes to the mountain. He cries. Then someone comes and says, this is my song, I'll help you." "Well then, I don't see any difference." "I am telling you there is no difference. Only the *dinihowi* that's for plain Indians like you and me, and the *damaagome* that's for doctors. . . . Well, I'll tell you, there is maybe some difference. The *damaagome* is kind of mean, quarrelsome, always fighting. The *dinihowi* is more peaceful."

There came a figure lurching toward us with a curious gait, something like an orangoutan, through the sagebrush. Robert Spring chuckled: "There comes your friend." Sure enough, it was Sukmit. "How did you know he and I were friends?" "Oh, Indians hear everything. It don't take long for news to travel in the sagebrush. I heard all about you stopping at his camp." Sukmit greeted me: "Hallo, Jaime!" (He was the only Pit River who ever called me by my first name. The others used my nickname in that country, Buckaroo Doc, or just Doc.) Then he and Robert Spring greeted each other: *Is, kaakaadzi* (Person, you are living). He sat down on one knee, which was his usual posture. "I heard Doctor Hall was sick, so I came to help," he said.

Now, that puzzled me. I had always heard that Indian shamans cordially detested each other. We told Sukmit that Hall had doctored himself and was now feeling better. "That's good," he said.

We all three went looking for the old man and found him sitting on a bench with his back to the shack and chewing tobacco. Robert Spring sat himself next to him and Sukmit and I on the ground in front, but careful to leave a clear space for the old blind man to spit into. Then there ensued the, to me, most amazing conversation about doctors and their poisons. Blind Hall started again on his pet subject of complaint: his pet *damaagome*, Jim Lizard, the lying sonofabitch he could never trust . . . but this time he had behaved himself, he wasn't mean enough to fool his own father when his father was sick, etc., etc. And Sukmit to corroborate: "Yes, some of them *damaagomes* is mean. When I started doctoring I tried a trick. I tried bringing my poison to a hand-game. Now, a doctor is not supposed to use his poison for gambling (this was addressed to me, not to Hall or Robert Spring). It's against the rules. But I thought I was smart, see. I thought to hell with the rules, I do like white man, see. Well, in the middle of the game I got awful thirsty, and I get up and go to the spring, and I take a long drink of water, and I got awful dizzy and sick, I got cramps, I puke. . . . See, my *damaagome* he do that, he mad because I bring him to hand-game, not supposed to do that." Blind Hall was roaring with laughter. "Ha, ha, ha. Your poison he make you sick. You bring him to hand-game, he make you sick. Ha, ha, ha."

Sukmit thought for a while, then he said: "Them *damaagomes* is dangerous things to handle. That's why I stick to my own and I don't try to steal other doctors' *damaagomes*. But this old man here, Doctor Hall, he don't care, he steal other doctors' *damaagomes*!" Blind Hall guffawed: "Sure I do! I steal other doctors' *damaagomes*. They steal mine, too, if they can. They try to steal my Raven, but he won't follow them. Ha, ha!" Sukmit said: "That's a good one, your Raven. I would like to have him myself. But I don't like to fool with other people's poisons.

31

It may be a bad one and you can't handle him and he make you sick." Blind Hall laughed again: "I am not afraid of them!"

Later on that day I asked Robert Spring: "How do the doctors steal each other's *damaagomes*?" "I dunno, Doc, I am not a doctor. But you heard Blind Hall say so himself. How do you steal another man's dog?"

I stayed a few days longer at that camp, then I decided to go back to Alturas and see if Jack Folsom was back at his place. I went north by Hantiyu. Toward evening I made my camp in a swale where there was a brook. There was another camp a few hundred yards upstream from me. After eating I strolled over there. Indians, a middle-aged man, a young woman, and a child. The man was surly: "What you want?" "Nothing. I just came to visit." "I don't want no visit! That's your camp over there. Stay over there. You come my country. You kill my people. You take my land. This is my camp. Leave me alone."

As I went the woman gave me an apologetic smile: "He cross fellow. He don't like white people." Anyone could see that.

I found Jack Folsom and Lena at their place. He told me that the Pit Rivers have a word for "year" and one for "month." The word for month is the same as that for moon, of course. What surprised me was that they use the same word (*tsulh*) for sun and moon; if they want to specify, they say "night *tsulh*" or "day *tsulh*."[2] They named the months: month of the groundhog; month of the squirrel; month of the wild turnips; month of the deer

---

[2] In the myths of many California tribes the moon is a man and the sun a woman. Among the Pit Rivers, however, I never heard either sun or moon mentioned in any stories or myths.

running, etc. They had twelve such months, and every fourth year they repeated the midwinter month (they were aware of the solstices). This was the occasion for a lot of quarreling. As Jack Folsom put it: "It used to get pretty stinky in the winter house, especially after Indians got dogs.[3] After two or three months of winter the litter of tules was lousy with vermin and fleas and bugs. People scratch all the time, want to get out go to the hills. Mebbe next moon is groundhog moon, and then next is squirrel moon, and then wild-turnip moon, that's the time people get out and go to the hills. They were in a hurry for the winter to end. And they argued and argued about it, the old men, the chiefs, did. This is the year we have to repeat the midwinter moon. No, it's next year. No, we did it three years ago. Ah, you don't know, you are too old, you are mixed up. We young fellows, we used to laugh listening to the old men argue. . . . Yes, Doc, the winters used to drag in the old-time *astsuy.* That's the time when you tell long stories, stories of long ago, *dilasini'qi* we call it. About Coyote, and Silver Fox, and Lizard, them all they used to be people, long long ago."

It was at about this time that I became acquainted with that "gambling" that I had been hearing so much about and which seemed to play such a part in Pit River life. It had puzzled me, for instance, to hear Jack Folsom lamenting the death of one of his sons a few years back, in these terms: "Yes, he was a fine boy, a good worker, never made any trouble, HE WAS A GOOD GAMBLER. . . ." Well, now I was going to have a chance to observe it; there was

---

[3]Dr. Merriam, the eminent zoologist, confirmed me in my opinion that the California Indians got their dogs rather recently, from other tribes (who presumably got theirs by European importation, like the horse).

going to be an Indian big-time at Tulu'kuupi, there would be lots of gambling. I had always thought of gambling as dice or roulette or fan-tan or what-have-you in man's everlasting effort to beat the mathematical laws of chance. And I could see that like all hoary manifestations of human imbecility it would always attract the charlatans and the crooks and the sharks, the whole setup which is associated in our minds with the words gambling and gambler. I was trying to fit that into the Indian picture; it didn't fit. . . .

Tulu'kuupi, the "sack," the end of the valley. Indians were converging from everywhere, in buggies, on horse-back, in wagons, and a few in rickety-rackety automobiles held up with bale-wire. Campfires everywhere in the sagebrush. There must have been a hundred or two hundred Indians. Greetings. Where is So-and-So? He is camped over there, under that juniper. . . . They say Wa'wa Eliyu is going to act as main chief. . . . Aw, he is too old. . . . The Paiutes have sent a team of good gamblers. And the Modocs, too. Some of our people are drunk already, the damfools, them Paiutes don't drink when they are playing hand-game, they'll beat us again. . . . I went around with Jack Folsom. He had more knowledge of modern ways than most of the older men, and it made him a sort of "chief." I knew quite a few Indians, from my previous experience as a cowboy in that country — and Jack introduced me to others: "He is all right. He is not a white man. He is Spanish." (In that part of the country, Spanish meant "Mexican," just riffraff to the white overlords of the ranches, only one degree above the Indians, who were on the level of horses and cattle.)

Evening had hardly set in when the rattle of sticks was heard, clack-clack-clack-clack-clack . . . and people began converging from all over the camp toward that spot. A

34

hand-game had started between a team of Paiutes on one side, and a mixed team of Modocs and Pit Rivers on the other.

Between them was a campfire. The men of each team were kneeling in a row — in front of them a long plank, just a board. The Paiutes at the moment "had the bones." So they were singing, and except for two of them who were hiding the bones, they all were beating on the board in front of them with short sticks. That was the clack-clack-clack I had heard. It was about as fast in time as the ticking of a watch. It was as uniform in time as a metronome, *and there was no beat*. The melody was a typical Paiute gambling-song, a short melody of four phrases, starting rather high and cascading down in intervals of a whole tone or a tone-and-a-half. They used the "closed throat" method of singing. There was no connection between the time of the clack-clack-clack and the time of the melody.

There they were singing away, the Paiutes were, and two of them were hiding the bones. The naked bone, and the tied bone. The tied bone has a string tied around its middle. You guess for the naked bone. But, if you are the guesser, you try to fool your enemy. You try to read his mind. You make melodramatic gestures. You point to the right, you point to the left, you point to the middle (with palm perpendicular), you point to the outside (there are *two* pairs of bones, remember, both naked bones might be outside). You try to remember this Paiute fellow's gambling habit, he always hides the naked bone in his left, and just as you say: "Ha," he shifts. You, you shifted them. You are supposed to turn your palms out. I did. No, you didn't. Yes I did. Where is the chief? He is drunk. Oh, what the hell, why don't you fellows play, you always argue —

A Pit River informant

. . . These sons-of-bitches *pahaqmaali* Paiutes, that fellow there . . . No, he is Modoc. . . . You are crazy, him a *lutuaami*? You are crazy, he is my, I call him *malis*. He is my brother-in-law. *Malis*, that's fire. So there is an argument started. Clack-clack-clack-clack at it again. The Modocs are hiding the bones, now. The Paiutes are guessing. They don't quarrel among themselves. They pull down their hats over their eyes. The Modocs and Pit Rivers are singing. They swing their bodies from left to right, in the rhythm of the song. But they are not swaying just right. Something is wrong. Two of them are very drunk. The Paiutes are putting their heads together, whispering, with their hats pulled over their eyes. Somebody throws a bunch of twigs on the fire. It blazes up. All the Paiutes grab their hats and shield their eyes. There is one fellow who seems to be their leader. He has a very dark face. His hair is down to his shoulders. They all are whispering to him. He leans over, listening to them. Sometimes he nods. The Modocs and Pit Rivers are getting a little bit out of hand. Two drunken fellows try to horn in. Suddenly they change their song. It falters for a while and dies away in the sagebrush. Everybody laughs. An old woman gets up and spits and goes to her camp in the darkness. Campfires everywhere around. People cooking. Smell of bacon. People calling across. "How is the game?" "Them Paiutes are winning. Our people are drunk. They have no luck, anyhow!"

That Paiute man starts. He claps his hands, then he spreads them apart. He is on his knees. Then he brings the hands together, slowly. He is pointing to the middle (both naked bones inside). One of the Pit Rivers shifts his bones. Everybody laughs. The Paiutes never laugh. They are very different people, full of the desert. An old woman cackles, back of the firelight. Now both players on the Modoc-Pit River combination get nervous and shift their bones. The Paiute man says: HA! and he points with an outstretched hand. Both Pit River-Modocs throw their bones across, laughing. A man bends over and pulls one of the markers and sticks it in the ground on the Paiute side. Everybody yells. He looks confused. "The bones are on that side. What's the matter with you?" He scoots out of sight. Now the Paiutes have the bones. . . .

I stirred in my sleep. The camp was quiet. Just a few babies crying here and there, but the game was going on, clack-clack-clack-clack, out there where the campfire was flickering and black shadows of men moving against it.

We were camped there nearly a week, playing hand-game, making speeches, long-winded speeches. Those speeches of the old men! You don't have to listen to them. Why do the young men sit there on the ground, listening with mouths agape? Nobody obliges them, no pressure of public opinion (there is very little public condemnation for anyone's sins, among the Pit Rivers, they are simply tolerant), then why do all the people, men, women, young men, even little boys, gather around, sit on the ground. Those speeches of the old men, those long-winded speeches!! They always start at the beginning of the world, literally: ". . . and then Silver Fox said to Coyote . . ." and it goes on and on and on. All the verbs are put in the remote past conjugation, with the ending in -*uaasa* or -*iaasa*). And then *kuan tsikuaasa dzeemul.* And then Coyote he didn't -*aasa* know what to answer. And if the white people get enough of us Indians to sign that paper for Washington, we will be like Coyote and we will -*aasa* lose the rest of our lands, etc., etc., etc. for hours. Then the people move over to another old man. He is a Pit

River by birth, but he was brought up by the Klamath Indians (who are first cousins to the Pit Rivers), and while there he came under the influence of two movements: the Indian Shakers and the Christian Missionaries (the C. M. failed utterly with the Pit Rivers, they didn't even get to first base). Now he starts. His speech is quite nonpolitical. It has to do with religion and Jesus. He speaks by turns in Pit River and in English: "This here Jesus, he and his wife Mary, and they had a little boy with them, they traveled all over the world, they made mountains and trees, they made trees, they made springs everywhere, *teeqaade toolol.* . . . This here Jesus he was a great man; he was the best gambler in the whole United States!" The Modocs weren't listening to him much; there were no Paiutes in the audience. Almost all the listeners were Pit Rivers. There were no jeers, no heckling, just a lot of brown faces squinting in the sun. When he was finished, mopping his brow, they moved over to where another hand-game had started, all women. There was a big Modoc woman. Nobody could guess her. She hid the bones in a bandanna handkerchief. While she sang she shook her big fat body, sitting on the ground, swaying from side to side with the rhythm of the song. Then she would whip her hands out with the handkerchief still in one hand. The guesser would yell "Ha." She would laugh, show the bones, and throw them in the air. They always guessed her wrong.

It was dawn, and everybody was stirring all over the camp. Some early wagons were already departing. Business of packing, gathering baskets, harnessing or saddling horses, calling scampering children. I was saddling my horse, talking to Jack Folsom. A man came to us. He was the same surly fellow who had received my visit so badly some time before. I had noticed him watching me closely around camp several times, but I never spoke to him and he never spoke to me. This man now came to me and he put a beautiful little buckskin bag embroidered with beads into my hands, and he said: "My wife made this for you." Then he just turned on his heel and was gone. I stood there, sort of dumbfounded. Jack Folsom looked at the bag and said: "That's nice bag, Doc, that's good work." "Who is that fellow, Jack?" "I don't know him, Doc. I think he comes from down the river."

From there I went back with Jack and Lena to their shack tucked away in the sagebrush, behind a hill not far from Alturas. We took up the study of language again, and went out in the brush with his rifle to shoot jackrabbits (hares) for the cooking pot. There were hundreds and hundreds of them, darting from every bush. In a minute or two we would bag one, which was enough for the three of us. Then we would sit down and talk and talk. . . . "Jack, have you got a *dinihowi*?" Jack looked at me, squinting a smile: "Where did you learn that word, Doc?" — "Oh, here and there, Blind Hall. . . ." Jack snorted. "That old bastard hasn't got any *dinihowis*. They wouldn't live with his poisons. You want to know what that old man does with *dinihowis*? He steals them, just like he steals other doctors' *damaagomes*. He steals honest Indians' *dinihowis* but he can't keep them. They won't live with his poisons. When he wants to get a woman he goes into the brush and he calls for a lice from her. . . ." "For a what?" "For a lice. Them things crawl around between your legs." "Oh, a louse." "I dunno. I always heard white people call them lice. We say *a'mits*. Lots of Indians got them. So this Hall goes into the bush, and he has got an *a'mits* himself for one of his poisons. And he gets his

40

a'mits to call for her *a'mits.* And pretty soon the woman
get up from her campfire, she don't know why but she go
wandering into the sagebrush and old Hall is there waiting
for her."

"But Jack, that lice is not her *damaagome!*" "How the
hell do I know it ain't her *damaagome.* It might be her
dinihowi. I didn't say it was her *damaagome.*"

"No, that's right, I made a mistake. I meant her
dinihowi."

"I didn't say it was her *dinihowi.* Lots of us got them
lice between our legs."

I shut up. Jack was a very kind man, but whenever I
seemed stupid he would sort of lose his temper and get
cross and squint across the hills. I had learned the weather
signals. So I shut up.

We were still sitting in the same spot. Jack says, out of
the blue: "Yes, I got a *dinihowi.* Must be a damn poor
Indian without a *dinihowi.* When I was a young fellow,
old people always get after us. You go get luck for yourself.
You can't live without luck. Go and run up the mountain
in the afternoon. Try to beat the sun, the red light, to the
top, get there first. Keep your breath. Run steady. . . . You
know, Doc, I used to be a good runner. We used to have
foot-races in the old-time days. All the young Indians we
used to try beat each other going from one place to
another, maybe five mile, maybe ten mile. Run through
the sagebrush, keep your breath in, don't slow down,
don't sit down and sleep, don't get scared, keep running
through the brush, sometimes awful high brush, higher
than your head. . . . I was pretty good runner in them
days. Now I make my race-horses run. . . . Well, the old
people kept after me. You beat the sun to the top of the
mountain, then you'll be a man. I tried, and I tried. Then

41

one day a big frog was standing in the road, right in the dust of the trail. He says: You'll never get to the top without me helping you. I been watching you. It's awful how hard you try. I'll help you. . . ."

"Did you get to the top that day?"

"Yes, I got to the top. There ain't nothing there."

"Then what?"

"Then I came down."

"Oh . . ."

"What do you mean, oh? I got my *dinihowi*, didn't I? I am always trying to tell you things, Doc, but you are worse than a young Indian."

We came back through the brush. He was wiping the barrel of the gun with a rope with a rag tied to it. I was carrying the hare of the day by the long ears. Lena was sitting in front of the shack. That woman was truly enormous. She was at her eternal beadwork. She looked up at us and smiled. Then she went back to her beads. I laid the hare in front of the campfire. Jack said, "Better draw it, Doc. We'll have it for supper. I am going out to look for them horses." Those were wonderful quiet days with Jack and Lena, in that little corner of sagebrush behind the turn of the hill.

But it was only a few days before Jack got restless again. He had some race-horses he had loaned to a fellow in Hat Creek. They were colts. He had to keep an eye on them. He didn't trust that fellow. Off they went again, in the spring-wagon, we pushed and hoisted and drug Lena into the wagon-bed where she sat enthroned amidst her many baskets. Jack got into the driver's seat, released the brakes. I didn't have time to say goodbye even. He had hitched up a colt with an old horse. The old horse started. The colt bucked. Down came the black snake over his buttocks. They were off and the wagon almost tipped, Lena was holding onto the sides, smiling. Jack turned his face around once. He was grinning and he yelled something, but I didn't catch what he said.

I stayed there that night, but in the morning I went.

2

I was up again, the next year. This time I had a jalopy, myself. Progress. You can't defend yourself against progress. So this time I came up following the Pit River from Redding up. I was meeting more and more Indians after Montgomery Creek. I had never been through that territory before, only once, years before with a drove of horses, through a snowstorm. I didn't even recognize the country.

I got into the upper land. It was getting dark. I had a wolfish-looking bitch swaying on the back, on top of my camping stuff. I was getting tired driving that damned car. I hate them. When I got to Big Valley I couldn't stand the driving over the rough road any more. I saw a campfire a little south of the road. I was awfully tired. I thought: They must be Indians.

I got out and walked over, being careful to make a noise. There was no need for care. There comes Sukmit: "I have been watching for you. I got lonesome for you. I sent my poison after you. The old lady is there, in the camp. Old lady Gordon died. The other woman, my uncle, she is dead. We are all going to die. We can't help it. What have you got there? Is that a coyote? Looks like a coyote. Don't growl at me, you son-of-a-bitch, I am Indian doctor. I ain't afraid of you. Want to be my poison? Say, Jaime, did you get my message? I got lonesome for you. You want to be a doctor? I teach you. I am Indian doctor. I teach you, pretty bad, get scared, I teach you, you no white man. . . ."

Under this avalanche I was being dragged across some wasteland toward the campfire I had seen. There were no introductions of any kind whatever. Nobody paid any attention to me at all. I sat in a corner. I said nothing. Then a little boy brought me a basket full of some kind of mush, and it had salt in it, too. I was reserved and very careful, keeping out of the way, in the outer light of the fire. Then Mary's chuckle came out of the darkness (I hadn't seen her until that moment, sitting there beyond the firelight): "Ha-ha, you white man."

I followed that bunch for several weeks. I never saw such a goddam lot of improbable people. Sukmit was the only acknowledged shaman, but he wasn't a leader. He was no chief, no *weheelu*, among them. We went around the brush. We would stop anywhere, evidently by common consent. We would stop in the brush. Always there was a spring near by. I never knew where we were going. We were going somewhere. I didn't care at all. We were going somewhere, maybe. And if we were not going somewhere,

Jaime de Angulo's touring car, on fieldtrip, around 1926.

we were not going, that's all. In the evening we would make a fire, several fires (there were several families of us). In the morning we moved again. I don't know where we were going. I don't think the Indians knew. We made quite a procession through the sagebrush, about six or seven of us, my car usually tagging at the end. I didn't know where we were going, nobody seemed to know where we were going, and then the night would settle on us, the fires would die down. The coyotes would begin barking from out in the brush. The Indians' dogs would howl back. Then everything would smolder back into the darkness.

Then one morning I was made to realize that there was something wrong about the white man's conception of the "taciturn" Indian. That happened the next day. We were going along the sagebrush, no road, just sagebrush, wind left, wind right, avoid this big clump, here's bad one, bump into the ditch . . . but there is no road at all anywhere, you are going through the brush, bumpety bump, all of us, six, seven, maybe eight cars, eight tin lizzies rattling through the sagebrush. Then, one morning, we had to stop. One of the tin lizzies was on the blink, and everybody got out to help. Then I witnessed something that amazed me. I had made up my mind that these men were straight out of the old Stone Age. I myself am not a mechanic; I hate machines; I am all thumbs; I don't understand machines; horses, yes; machines, no. And here I was watching these Stone Age men unscrew and rescrew and take things apart or out of the engine and spread them on a piece of canvas on the ground . . . but the amazing thing to me was their argumentation. It was perfectly logical. " . . . Can't be the ignition, look, I get a spark . . . I tell you, it's in the transmission. . . . Now pull that lever. . . ." Maybe I was overimpressed because the simplest machine smells of magic to me. Maybe I missed a lot of their argument because off and on they would lapse into Pit River. They called the battery *hadatsi* "heart"; a wheel is *pi'nine* (a hoop used in the old days for target practice); and so on a and so forth. But certainly they made use of logic just as any white man would. Finally the engine, or whatever was wrong, was repaired. Then I overheard one young fellow say to another: "You know why this happened? Because he has been sleeping with his woman while she was menstruating! That against the rules."

At last everything was fixed: the engine put together again, everything rescrewed . . . but the trek of the tin lizzies was not resumed. We just stayed there.

I don't know why we stayed there. We just stayed there, in the middle of nowhere, in the middle of the sagebrush. After that car which had broken down had been repaired, I naturally expected that everybody would get back into their cars, and the procession be resumed. But no, nobody got back into the cars; everybody was drifting around, sitting here, sitting there, gossiping, yawning.

I asked a man: "Are we going on, or do we camp here?" He answered: "I dunno. I am not the chief. Ask that old man over there." I went to the old man over there. He said he was not the chief. Ask that fellow over there. That fellow over there was a middle-aged man. He said: "Hell, I am not the one to say, I am not a chief!" "Well, who is a chief here?" "I dunno. That old man over there, I guess. He is old enough to have the say. Go and ask him." That old man over there was the same old man over there, and he gave me the same treatment. He was no chief. Who said he was a chief? They could start when they liked, when they jolly well liked, he didn't care, he didn't even know where they were going, where the hell were they going, did they know where they were going, did I know where they were going??...He sat on the foot-board of one of the cars. He was squinting into the afternoon sun; it was late afternoon, by then. He was chewing tobacco and spitting the brown juice. He paid no more attention to me and went back to his reverie, squinting into the sun.

I noticed a woman had started a campfire. Very soon another one did likewise. So I went to my car and drove it next to Sukmit's. Old Mary was sitting on the ground in the shade of the car, weaving a rough basket of willow twigs. "Where is Sukmit?" "*Tsesuwi diimas'adi*, I don't know, went off in the brush some place, that boy is crazy, *yalu'tuusi*, always looking for *damaagomes*; you bring me firewood, white man, I cook." "All right."

The sun was going down. I heard two or three shots, off in the sagebrush. I made our fire. There were four or five other campfires. A man came by; he had several hares by the ears; he tossed one over to us. Mary drew it, threw the guts to my bitch, hacked it in four pieces, and stuck these on sticks to broil over the fire. No sight of Sukmit. We ate. Then Mary told me an old-time story. I spread my blankets on the ground. I rolled a cigarette and watched the stars. Some coyotes started a howling, not far off. My bitch stood up, all bristles, and she howled back (in answering coyotes, most dogs howl instead of barking). I went to sleep with my head full of old-time stories, tin lizzies, *damaagomes* mixed up with engines, coyotes and sagebrush.

I was awakened by the usual quarrel between Sukmit and his mother. The smell of coffee was in the air. We ate.

I observed the camp. There were no preparations for starting. Everybody lolling around. Mary took up her basket and kept on weaving. Another woman went to the spring with a bucket (there was a spring, nearby; of course they must have known). A man was tinkering with his car. Another one went off into the brush with his gun. That old man, the supposed "chief," was going around poking at things with a stick. He was almost blind. The morning was drawing on. I took out my notebook and started working on linguistics.

The days went by. Not so many days, but four, five days, maybe. I don't remember exactly. I was not taking notes. I was living. Sagebrush. Old-time stories, hares cooking over the fire, slow gossip, So-and-So is poisoning So-and-So, I don't believe it, yes he is, how do you know, well his paternal aunt belongs to the *hammaawi*, and they poisoned his *apau*. "That doesn't make him related!" "Who said related? I didn't say related. I said they poisoned him.". . . The days went by, four, five, six days.

Then it happened. It was midday, or near. I heard a man say, way off: *"S. huptsiidzima."* If he had said *lhuptiidza toolol*, "Let's all go," it would have been different. But no, it was not in the imperative mode, it was in the indicative: "We are going, all of us, *toolol*, we are going, *s. huptsiidzima*, we are all going." He didn't say: LET'S ALL GO! No, he merely stated a fact: WE ARE ALL GOING.

It was like a whirlwind. I turned around. Women were throwing baskets into the tin lizzies. Then without any further warning or consultation one of the tin lizzies started off in a cloud of dust. Another was right on its heels. Then a third one, but this one had hardly started when someone yelled: "Hey! you are forgetting your baby!!" The car backed, a young woman jumped out and

50

ran to a juniper tree where the baby was sleeping in the cradle-board swinging under a branch; she slung the cradle-board over her shoulder and ran back to the car, laughing and laughing; everybody was laughing; then the car started again.

Sukmit yelled at me: "*Lhupta*, let's go! For Christ's sake, are you going to stay here forever?!" I picked up my papers and ran for my own car. . . . We go, we go, we wind in and out, all afternoon, all the cars more or less following each other, we skirted the town of Alturas, never stopped, we were going north, the sun went down, there was a moon, we kept going, somehow or other no car broke down, not even a flat tire, we had luck with us, and toward morning we stopped on those flats by Davis Creek. . . .

I was going back to Berkeley. I wasn't going to be caught by the fall, much less by the winter (it goes down to minus 30 Fahrenheit all over the plateau, Alturas, Susanville, Lakeview). I said to Sukmit: "Let's go down southward. I have a camping-place there in Berkeley. It's close to San Francisco." "Yes, I have heard of that place. Lots of people, they say." "Well, let's go, *lhepta*, you and me." "No, not *lhepta*, *lhupta*. We are not going home, we are going away from home. I have told you that a million times already. It's no use trying to teach a white man." "I am going to my home," I yelled. "My home, that's *septa*, isn't it?" "No, it isn't *septa*. That would mean that you are on your way. You are sitting here, ain't you? You are not *septa*, you are *tapte-gudzii*. . . ." The old lady called over from the fire: "What you two arguing about again? You all the time the two of you arguing like two old men! You white man he Indian, ha-ha-ha. . . ."

51

We sit down under that tall pine tree, and eat. We are still quarreling, Sukmit and I. "How can you go southward and leave your *damaagome* behind you?" "He can find me, can't he? I can sing his song. he'll hear it. Just like 'lectricity, goes under ground, anywhere I can call my *damaagome*, he comes. . . ." Old Mary looks up. "He never come. . ." she says. Sukmit flares into a rage at her. "He come! He come! He come! He is stamping around her. He is in a perfect rage. He is shaking both fists over her head. She says: "He never come."

I was sort of upset, even shocked, by this childish behavior, this tantrum, on his part. There he was the powerful shaman, the tamer of *damaagomes, trépignant autour de sa mère*, shaking his fists over her head, shouting: "They'll come! They'll come when I call them, goddam it they'll come!!" The old lady was sitting on the ground weaving her basket. She smiled; she kept repeating calmly: "They won't come. . .too far. . .they can't hear you."

After a while he calmed down. I proposed to record some songs on my phonograph machine. I carried around one of those old Edison phonographs with a big horn. You made the records on wax cylinders with a special cutting jewel needle; then to play them you changed to a needle with a rounded point. The whole contraption was crude and primitive compared to modern methods. It was hard enough to operate in a laboratory; imagine it in the open, competing with the wind; the horn would swing around; we cursed. . . .How I sweated and labored over those Indian songs, and the fortune I spent on broken records!. . .That was before the days of amplification; later on new methods appeared; flat disks, unbreakable and permanent; wonderful improvements. . .but the Indians are gone, no more singing to record.[4]

Sukmit had a powerful voice of which he was vain. He was delighted to sing into the horn and then hear his own voice thrown back to him. We recorded several songs, mostly gambling songs and some puberty-dance songs. Then he said: "Let's record Old Blind Hall's medicine-song, you know, that one about digging up wild turnips and they all are rotten." So we put that on. It goes something like this:

> *At Dalmo'ma near the spring*
> *I dig for wild turnips*
> *At Dalmo'ma in the evening*
> *I turn up but rotten ones.*

Then I said to him: "Sukmit, let's record one of your own medicine-songs." The old lady had heard me, and she cried from where she was sitting at the campfire. "Don't do it, Sukmit, don't do it, *tse-dutsee, tse-dutsee*!!" He seemed dubious, torn two ways by his vanity and his fear of possible consequences. "See, suppose I put my song in the machine; now you go to Berkeley; sometime you play my song; my *damaagome* he hear it, he say: Ha! my father is calling me, I'd better go and find him, maybe he needs me. . . . So he come here to Berkeley, strange place, maybe he get lost, maybe somebody steal him . . . then I get sick, maybe I die. . . ." "Aw! he couldn't hear that phonograph all the way from Alturas!" "Sure he can! Just like 'lectricity,

---

[4]The University would not help me; took no interest; would not even give me enough money to have the records transcribed and made permanent on modern disks. Decent anthropologists don't associate with drunkards who go rolling in ditches with shamans.

it goes underground, but it don't need no wires."[5] "What do you know about electricity?! Electricity doesn't work that way!" "Hell, what do you know about *damaagomes*? You are nothing but a white man, a goddam tramp."[6] "No, I am not a white man!" "Yes, you are a white man, you are a white man forever!!"

Old Mary chuckled from over the campfire "You two always quarreling like two old men. You Indian, you white man, ha-ha-ha! You both crazy!"

So I took them down to Berkeley in my auto, Sukmit and old Mary (she once told me her Indian name; it had something to do with tule reeds at dawn; but I never heard anyone call her by it; Sukmit called her *niini*, baby-talk for *nen* "mother"; and I also called her that after a while; other Indians called her "aunt," or "sister-in-law on the brother's side," which is *wattulaawi*, or whatever the relationship term.

The city was a great disappointment to Sukmit. Didn't interest him at all. "Too many people crawling around just like ants — makes me crazy. . . ." He spent most of his time wandering in the hills back of the University campus. He looked sad and dejected. He didn't quarrel any more.

One day I said to him: "Sukmit, I know what's troubling you. . . . You have been wandering in the hills and calling your *damaagomes*, and they don't hear you!" He looked at me and I thought he was going to burst into

---

[5] This was before the days of wireless (at least before wireless became common knowledge) — an interesting example of so-called "primitive mentality."

[6] The Pit Rivers call the whites *enellaaduwi*, literally "wanderer," from the verbal root *—Ilaa—* "to wander," plus the adverbial suffix *—duw—* "around." What struck the Pit Rivers most about the first whites (prospectors, trappers, etc.) was that they appeared to be homeless.

Sukmit in Berkeley

tears. "Yes," he said, "you and *niini*, you were right; they don't hear me; they don't come! I am going to die if I stay here."

So I sent them back on the train. Funny-looking pair they made at the station, bewildered, he with his long hair and his black sombrero, his long arms and his hump; she clutching a bundle; and her gray hair under a bright silk handkerchief we had just bought for her.

I spoke a word to the conductor for them. He smiled broadly: "Sure I'll take care of them. I know Indians. I was raised in Oklahoma."

As the train pulled out, old Mary gave me the Pit River goodby: *Is tus'i taakaadzee*, Man, live well! *Ittu toolol hakaadzi-gudzuma*, We also will live.

3

I went up north again the next summer. I found Jack
Folsom and Lena at their place behind the little hill in the
sagebrush. I noticed that Lena seemed apathetic, ill, Jack
was as usual, with his quizzical smile, his quiet ways, his
practical sense. "Say, Doc, I hear your friend Sukmit is
around. There is a woman sick near town, you know, that
place just before you reach town, Indians live there, well,
there is a woman sick there, some doctor poisoned her,
and they got your friend Sukmit to doctor her . . . and say,
Doc, we are pretty near out of grub, you will be in town
in two minutes with your car, today is Saturday and the
stores will be open late, and will you bring back some
grub, get some bacon, and bring some sweets for Lena,
she loves sweets, I don't know what's the matter with that

woman, Doc, something's wrong, she don't look well to me." "All right, Jack."

So I went to Alturas, did the shopping, and on the way back, it was dusk, I saw the familiar figure of Sukmit, a little way off the road, walking through the brush with long strides. I stopped the car, and honked and yelled. He paid no attention. I honked and yelled again. Surely he must hear me. I got out of the car and went up to him. He had heard me all right, and he was in a towering rage: "Goddam you, I am fixing for a doctoring! I have caught a new *damaagome* and I am training him, he is wild yet, he was following me like a dog, and here you come yelling your head off, you scared him away!" "I am sorry, Sukmit, I didn't know. . . ." "You never know anything. You'll never learn anything, you'll never be an Indian, you'll always be a damfool white man!!" "All right, all right, you don't have to be so nasty about it," and I turned to go. He followed me: "Well, aren't you going to give me a ride? They are waiting for me, I have to doctor a sick woman." "What's the use if I scared your *damaagome*?" "Do you think I have only one *damaagome*? That's just a new one I am training."

So I took him to the place. There were a dozen or so Indians gathered around a campfire. There was a woman lying under a blanket on a bed of tules on the ground. Old Mary was there. She greeted me with her usual banter: "Here is the Indian white man. He is going to do the interpreting. No, maybe he'll do the doctoring. Ha-ha-ha, Indian white man." Most of the Indians already knew me. Greetings. "*Is kaakaadzi*, Man, you are alive, *is kaakaadzi*. Where have you been? Where is your wife, your son, *mi'mu amiteudzan, mi'mu belatsi*? Why didn't they come?"

Sukmit looked somber and abstracted. He went and

looked at the sick woman silently; then he came back and knelt in front of the fire. Old Mary then got up and went a little way into the sagebrush and called the *damaagomes*.[7] Everybody became silent. Then Sukmit started one of his songs. Two or three people caught on, then others, then nearly everybody. Then he clapped his hands and the singing stopped abruptly. Now he is interpellating a poison, and old Mary, his mother, interprets (that is, repeats word for word, but more slowly, although Sukmit never got himself into a state of *bafouillage*, like Blind Hall and some others). And so on and so forth. In between interpellations of the poisons there was the usual relaxing and smoking by the audience and the usual gossip. But Sukmit never relaxed. He became more and more somber and abstracted. To me he seemed to be getting exhausted. After a while of this he got up and "sucked" the sick woman: he put his lips to different parts of her body and sucked with a strong hissing noise. Then he came back and knelt again in front of the fire, right next to me. He looked very sick. He asked for a container. Somebody passed him an empty can that had contained lard (a three-pound can), and he puked and puked and puked into it. I was right next to him. What he puked looked exactly like very dark blood, but the light was uncertain. He made a grimace and said to me: "Fuahh!. . . it looks like coffee." He was still retching. He poured the can into the fire.[8]

[7]After the *damaaagomes* have been called, no one is allowed to approach the meeting, whether Indian or white man. The reason is obvious: the sudden arrival of a stranger might scare away the *damaagomes* hovering in the air over the shaman's head.

[8]The can looked about half full. Was it an intestinal hemorrhage of hysterical origin? Sukmit (unlike some of the shamans, Old Modoc Kate, for instance, of whom I will speak later) was incapable of *supercherie*. I can vouch for that. I knew him too well. When two boon companions get drunk together time and time again, the truth is bound to come out. I simply have no explanation for the stuff in that can except the one given above.

Most of the Indians then left. Old Mary looked very tired also. She said to me: "You take care of your Sukmit," and she disappeared. Sukmit was like a drunken man. I spread my blankets on the ground and dragged him in after me. For a long time he was crying like a child, and shaking all over. Finally he went to sleep.

In the morning he was quite all right. So also was the sick woman (she evidently had had a bad case of "funk"). She came to where we were having breakfast, and she gave Sukmit a string of beads for payment. She said: "It's not much but I am a poor woman." Sukmit took the string and threw it to his mother, and he said to the woman: "That's good. I am not doing it for payment." Then Sukmit pumped up his tires and he and old Mary started for Big Valley (which was their home), and I went back to Jack and Lena at their place in the sagebrush around the little hill.

Poor Lena was really sick. Jack would have liked to call in Blind Hall, but he was away somewhere down river. Then we heard that a bunch of Modocs was in town on their way to their home in Oregon, and with them was old Kate, a famous medicine-woman, and Jack decided to try her. She arrived in the afternoon, in a horse-wagon, with her son, a big strapping fellow (with whom I later studied the Modoc language). She was a little bit of an old old woman, so *racroquevillée* that she was almost bent double; she was nearly blind; still she insisted on "helping" (all the conversation had to be in English, since the Modocs didn't understand Pit River, and vice versa) with the cooking. She would totter around, extend a claw, peer, grab something and drop it in the skillet. Jessie (Jack's daughter by another wife — and a big, handsome woman Jessie was, somewhere around in her forties, graceful, dignified, a little bit haughty), who had come to help,[9] Jessie would sigh, turn her face aside to grimace, then calmly remove whatever *immondice* old Kate had dropped into the skillet.

Evening arrived. Old Kate had a sister who acted as her "interpreter," a much younger woman. Everything was ready; we were all inside the cabin; still old Kate was waiting for something; finally she said: "Dat white man going to stay?" "He is no white man!" said Jack. "He is Indian just like us." "What tribe?" she asked me. "Spanish," I answered. "Oh, dat's all right. Spanish good people." To her, too, Spanish meant Mexican.

Old Kate's procedure was slightly different from Blind Hall, Sukmit, or the other Pit River shamans I have associated with; but on the whole it followed the same lines — perhaps a little less loose, a trifle more conventionalized. For instance, her songs appeared to be directed less to an individual *damaagome* than to a generalized animal. Her sister would explain to me: "That's duck song. . . that's crane song. . . that's pelican song. . . ." The old woman's son had gone out. Doctoring didn't interest him. The Pit Rivers didn't know that kind of singing and were too self-conscious to try. Only the old woman's sister carried on the singing. Old Kate complained. Finally she turned to me: "Why you no sing? *Canta, canta!*" "All right, I'll try." The songs weren't difficult. They had more lilt than the Pit River ones. Anyhow, the important thing was to make a noise and be heard by the poisons.

Toward midnight or one o'clock (unlike the Pit River shamans, who never doctor for more than a couple of

---

[9]Lena had raised Jessie, but they must have been almost the same age, at most ten years' difference — so Jessie looked upon Lena as her mother.

hours, Kate kept it up all night, right till dawn — although all the Pit Rivers had fallen asleep in various corners), Kate had a fit. She started to shake, foam at the mouth, and throw herself around. At first her sister tried to hold her down, but she wasn't strong enough. She called for help to the Pit Rivers; but for some reason no one moved. Then she yelled at me: "Hey, you Mexican, hold her, I'll call her son. . . ." He came in, a calm, big, powerful fellow. Yet, with the two of us sitting on her she managed once to free herself, that little bit of an old woman whom ordinarily you could have pushed over with your little finger! After a while she quieted down, and the singing started again, at intervals. But she was tired. Once she peered at the roof: "Is dat morning?" "No, Kate, it's the moon. There is a crack in the roof." She sighed.

Finally she started to extract the poison. She sucked and sucked. Then she straightened up, put her hand to her mouth, and grabbed something that was between her teeth. In the light of the lamp I saw distinctly what she did: she bit a piece of her own fingernail off. This she exhibited around as the poison. Then she called for a bowl of water; she drowned the poison in it and threw the water in a corner of the room.

In the morning the Modocs started to go. Jack Folsom wanted to give Kate some money, but she refused it, "I didn't do any good, Jack, you people don't sing, my poison no hear. Your woman going to die. Too bad." She said goodby to me. "You good man, Spanish, you help, you sing. Come see me my place Oregon." I said I would.

(I did go there, the next year, to study the Modoc language with her son. I had many talks with her. One day I was sitting on a log in the sun beside her; she was smoking her pipe; I said: "Kate, you remember that time

62

Jack Folsom (r) talking to Jaime de Angulo, Berkeley

at Jack Folsom's place when you doctored that woman. . . . You bit off your fingernail and said it was the poison. . . ." She gave me a sidelong look, pretty piercing in spite of her rheumy eyes; she grumbled: ". . . You know too much — sure dat's tomfoolery, good for people, make him believe — but my poison him no fool, him powerful, no nonsense, but he no hear dat time, son-of-a-bitch!" ". . . Kate, why did you become a doctor?" "Oh, long time ago, me young girl, go in woods look for berries, I no look for poison, poison find me." "Did he scare you?" "You bet he scare me!" "Does he still scare you when he comes?" She burst into her cackling laughter; "Hell NO! He don't scare me. I scare him now!!!")

Soon after the Modocs left, Lena's own father arrived from Hat Creek country. His name was Jack Wilson. He drove in in a horse-wagon, and with him was an "elder brother" (or cousin) of his, who must have been close to ninety or a hundred; Jack Folsom (who didn't know his own age by years) said of Bob-Chief, or Tom-Chief (like all Indians he had a variety of American names): "When I was a young fellow that old man had already buried three wives." He was still erect, but walked slowly; his skin was the color of chocolate; a few long white whiskers made him look like a walrus.

Jack Wilson was a "sort of doctor," according to Jack Folsom. He would doctor his own daughter, that night. Old Tom-Chief would interpret. Jack Wilson was a tall man, very silent. During the day Tom-Chief, who usually sat on a log, would totter into the sagebrush and make a sort of speech. "What is he doing?" I asked Jack. "Oh, he is telling old-time stories, what the people used to do long ago." "But there is nobody there. To whom is he talking?" Jack shrugged his shoulders: "To the sagebrush, I guess."

When evening came, old Tom-Chief went out and called the *damaagomes*. Three young Indians had arrived; but they were slightly drunk. They sang a *contre-temps* and laughed. Jack had to reprimand them. Old Tom was very deaf; he didn't hear what the doctor said; so everybody had to shout at him what the shaman had said so he could repeat it; the whole thing was a failure. After about an hour Jack Wilson gave up in despair. "No use! My poison don't hear. Mountain lion, wolf, too far away, don't hear!"

In the morning he said to me: "I lost all my children. This is the last one. I lose her too."

It was in the afternoon. Autumn and warm. The door of the cabin stood open. Away to the west I could see the hills of sagebrush, silent, and the mountains beyond. One of those days that do not move. There were half a dozen of us in the cabin, and the sick woman breathing heavily on her pile of blankets. I don't know how we all knew it, but we all felt that she was dying just then. At last, Jack Folsom broke down. He buried his face in his hands and started to cry. He cried like a little child, with convulsive sobs. Then that awful sound of the rattle. And even before that had died away Jessie began the wail. Oh, that weird, wild, atrocious thing that goes mounting like the shriek of a wounded beast, that infernal yell drawn away until it falls in a series of exhausted sobs. And again, and again. I was to hear that wail all night through the sagebrush until it drove me mad.

The old man, her father, was kneeling at her head. His face twitched uncontrollably. He closed her eyes, and laid a handkerchief over her face. Then he, too, broke down. He took the head of his child in his lap, he raised it to his breast, and he sobbed and sobbed.'

All night long Jessie wandered through the brush, wailing, wailing. And all through the night Indians kept arriving. The men sat against the wall. The women went out into the night and wailed.

One Indian is dead.

Then Jack took his wife's body away to bury it in Hat Creek, her home. He said to me: "I'll be back here in about two weeks, and then we will burn her. Will you stay here for me, Doc?"

I was sort of puzzled about this business of burying first, and burning her after, but I didn't ask him any questions. I said I would stay until he got back. He said: "You sure you won't be scared?" "No, . . . why should I?" "Account of the woman who died." "But why?" "She might come and kill you by mistake." "Hell no!" I said.

The very night after they had left, Wild Bill arrived. He was a horse-breaker by trade and I had known him in the days of my venture in ranching. A delightful fellow, always full of fun and jokes, and a superb rider; in fact he was a crazy daredevil. We had always been friends.

I was surprised to see him. He had tied his horse to a post in the corral and came over to me. He said he had come for the funeral, and that the woman-who-had-died was his cousin. He said "sister."

"How can she be your sister, Bill?"

"Well, she is, Indian way."

"I don't see how."

"Oh, yes. Look: her *apun*, her grandfather on the mother side was the elder brother, what we call *apau*, to my sister, the younger than me, my *enun*."

"But Bill, that doesn't make her your sister!"

"Sure it does, Doc. . . . See, if a man is my wife's brother I call him *malis*, and my own brother, if he is older I call him *apau*, but if he is younger I call him *atun*. Just like my sister, *apis* or *enun*. But if he is my uncle, if he is my father's sister, then I call him . . . Oh, hell, Doc; you can't get it straight in English . . . But I tell you, this woman who died she is related to me, I know, because she always called this here Tom-Chief, *aqun*, and he also called me *aqun*, and that proves it."

Wild Bill said he would stay here and wait for Jack Folsom and the rest of the party to come back from the *atsuge* country. That evening he told me a lot about Coyote and the Coyote saga. The Coyote stories form a regular cycle, a saga. This is true of all of California; and it extends eastward even as far as the Pueblos of Arizona and New Mexico. Coyote has a double personality. He is at once the Creator, and the Fool. This antinomy is very important. Unless you understand it you will miss the Indian psychology completely — at least you will miss the significance of their literature (because I call their tales, their "old-time stories," literature).

The wise man and the buffoon: the two aspects of Coyote, Coyote Old Man. Note that I don't call them the good and the evil, because that conception of morality does not seem to play much part in the Pit River attitude to life. Their mores are not much concerned with good and evil. You have a definite attitude toward moral right and moral wrong. I don't think the Pit River has. At least, if he has, he does not try to coerce. I have heard Indians say: "That's not right what he is doing, that fellow . . ." "What d'you mean it's not right?" ". . . Well . . . you ain't supposed to do things that way . . . it never was done that way . . . there'll be trouble." "Then why don't you stop him?" "Stop him? How can I stop him? It's his way."

The Pit Rivers (except the younger ones who have gone to the Government School at Fort Bidwell) don't ever seem to get a very clear conception of what you mean by the term God. This is true even of those who speak American fluently, like Wild Bill. He said to me: "What is this thing that the white people call God? They are always talking about it. It's goddam this and goddam that, and in the name of the god, and the god made the world. Who is that god, Doc? They say that Coyote is the Indian God, but if I say to them that God is Coyote, they get mad at me. Why?"

"Listen, Bill, tell me . . . Do the Indians think, really think that Coyote made the world? I mean, do they really think so? Do you really think so?"

"Why of course I do. . . . Why not? . . . Anyway . . . that's what the old people always said . . . only they don't all tell the same story. Here is one way I heard it: it seems like there was nothing everywhere but a kind of fog. Fog and water mixed, they say, no land anywhere, and this here Silver Fox. . . . "

"You mean Coyote?"

"No, no, I mean Silver Fox. Coyote comes later. You'll see, but right now, somewhere in the fog, they say, Silver Fox was wandering and feeling lonely. *Tsikuellaaduwi maandza tsikualaasa.*[10] He was feeling lonely, the Silver Fox. I wish I would meet someone, he said to himself, the Silver Fox did. He was walking along in the fog. He met Coyote. 'I thought I was going to meet someone,' he said.

---

[10]When you tell old-time stories of long ago, every verb must begin with *tsik* —, which then is more or less blended with the pronominal prefix.

The Coyote looked at him, but he didn't say anything. 'Where are you traveling?' says Fox. 'But where are YOU traveling? Why do you travel like that?' 'Because I am worried.'[11] 'I also am wandering,' said the Coyote, 'I also am worrying and traveling.' 'I thought I would meet someone, I thought I would meet someone. Let's you and I travel together. It's better for two people to be traveling together, that's what they always say. . . .' "

"Wait a minute, Bill. . . . Who said that?"

"The Fox said that. I don't know who he meant when he said: *that's what they always say.* It's funny, isn't it? How could he talk about *other* people since there had never been anybody before? I don't know. . . I wonder about that sometimes, myself. I have asked some of the old people and they say: That's what I have been wondering myself, but that's the way we have always heard it told. And then you hear the Paiutes tell it different! And our own people down the river, they also tell it a little bit different from us. Doc, maybe the whole thing just never happened. . . . And maybe it did happen but everybody tells it different. People often do that, you know. . . . "

"Well, go on with the story. You said that Fox had met Coyote. . . ."

"Oh, yah. . . Well, this Coyote he says: "What are we going to do now?' 'What do you think?' says Fox. 'I don't know,' says Coyote. 'Well then,' says Fox, 'I'll tell you: LET'S MAKE THE WORLD.' 'And how are we going to do that?' 'WE WILL SING,' says the Fox.

"So, there they were singing up there in the sky. They

---

[11] To be worried, *—inismallauw—* (conjugation II). When an Indian is worried, he goes wandering, *—inillaaduw—.* When he is "wandering" he goes around the mountains, cries, breaks pieces of wood, hurls stones. Some of his relatives may be watching him from afar, but they never come near.

were singing and stomping[12] and dancing around each other in a circle. Then the Fox he thought in his mind: CLUMP OF SOD, come!! That's the way he made it come: *by thinking.*[13] Pretty soon he had it in his hands. And he was singing, all the while he had it in his hands. They were both singing and stomping. All of a sudden the Fox threw that clump of sod, that *tsapettia,*[14] he threw it down into the clouds. 'Don't look down!' he said to the Coyote. 'Keep on singing! Shut your eyes, and keep them shut until I tell you.' So they kept on singing and stomping around each other in a circle for quite a while. Then the Fox said to the Coyote: 'Now, look down there. What do you see?' 'I see something...I see something...but I don't know what it is.' 'All right. Shut your eyes again!' Now they started singing and stomping again, and the Fox thought and wished: Stretch! Stretch! 'Now look down again. What do you see?' 'Oh! it's getting bigger!' 'Shut your eyes again and don't look down!' And they went on singing and stomping up there in the sky. 'Now look down again!' 'Oooh! Now it's big enough!' said the Coyote.

"That's the way they made the world, Doc. Then they both jumped down on it and they stretched it some more. Then they made mountains and valleys; they made trees

---

[12]Indian dancing is not like the European, by lifting the heels and balancing the body on the toes; on the contrary, one foot is raised *flat* from the ground while the other foot is pressed into the ground (by flexing the knee); then a very slight pause with one foot in the air; then the other foot is stamped flat into the ground while the first one is lifted. That is the fundamental idea; there are many variations; besides, the shoulders and head are made to synchronize or syncopate.

[13]I am not romancing, nor translating loosely; *hay-dutsi-la* means literally "by thinking." The radical *hay* — means "thought"; *dutsi* is the verb "to be" used here as an auxiliary in participial form (i.e. "being"); —*la* is the suffix representing the instrumental case (i.e. "by").

[14]Those big clumps of coarse grass and sod which gradually rise above the level of the water on the marshes are called *tsappetia.*

and rocks and everything. It took them a long time to do all that!"

"Didn't they make people, too?"

"No. Not people. Not Indians.[15] The Indians came much later, after the world was spoiled by a crazy woman, Loon. But that's a long story. . . . I'll tell you some day."

"All right, Bill, but tell me just one thing now: there was a world now; then there were a lot of animals living on it, but there were no people then. . . . "

"Whad'you mean there were no people? Ain't animals people?"

"Yes, they are . . . but . . . "

"They are not Indians, but they are people, they are alive . . . Whad'you mean animal?"

"Well . . . how do you say 'animal' in Pit River?"

" . . . I dunno. . . . "

"But suppose you wanted to say it?"

"Well . . . I guess I would say something like *teeqaade-wade toolol aakaadzi* (world-over, all living) . . . I guess that means animals, Doc."

"I don't see how, Bill. That means people, also. People are living, aren't they?"

"Sure they are! that's what I am telling you. Everything is living, even the rocks, even that bench you are sitting on. Somebody *made that bench for a purpose*, didn't he? Well then *it's alive*, isn't it? Everything is alive. That's what we Indians believe. White people think everything is dead. . . . "

"Listen, Bill. How do you say 'people'?"

"I don't know . . . just *is*, I guess."

"I thought that meant 'Indian.' "

---

[15]The word for "people" is *is*. Nowadays it is applied especially to Indians, in contradistinction to the term applied to the whites: *enellaaduwi.*

71

"Say . . . Ain't we *people*?!"

"So are the whites!"

"Like hell they are!! We call them *inillaaduwi*, 'tramps,' nothing but tramps. They don't believe anything is alive. They are dead themselves. I don't call that 'people.' They are smart, but they don't know anything. . . . Say, it's getting late, Doc, I am getting sleepy. I guess I'll go out and sleep on top of the haystack. . . ."

"But you'll die of cold! It's already freezing, these nights."

"Naw, I won't. I am an Indian. I am used to it."

"But why don't you sleep here, inside?"

"WHAT?! Are you crazy? That woman might come and kill me."

"You mean Lena?"

"Shh! . . . Doc! For God's sake don't call her, don't call her name! Just say: the woman who died. That's bad enough. She is probably somewhere around, somewhere around here. They haven't burnt her things yet, you know, her baskets, her blankets, her clothes . . . all these things are calling her, are calling her shadow, her *de'lamdzi*."

"But why should she hurt you?"

"She don't want to hurt me."

"But you just said she might kill you. . . ."

"Well, she'll take my shadow away with her, and then I'll die."

"What for would she take your shadow away with her?"

"Oh, to keep from getting lonely on the road to the land of the dead people."

"Where is that?"

"I dunno. Nobody knows. Somewhere out west. They say there is a big lake there, no end to it, and the dead people live there on an island . . . I dunno . . . that's what I've heard."

"But, Bill, I still don't see why she should want to take you there. . . ."

"I just told you, Doc: to keep from getting lonely on the trip to the land of the dead. You would do the same thing yourself if you were going to a strange place. You would take along someone you knew and liked."

"Well then, she might take me, Bill. I know she liked me."

"Sure! That's why I tell you that you are a damn fool to sleep here!"

"Listen, Bill, tell me something else before you go . . . about the shadow, what do you call it, the *dalilamdzi?*"

"Naw, that means 'to make a shadow,' for instance *salilamdzi*, that means I am making a shadow, *kalilamdzi* it's you who are making a shadow. . . . No, Doc, I know what you are thinking about, that's the *de'lamdzi*, the shadow, that's not the same as *dalilamdzi*, that's the shadow . . . oh, hell, I dunno what's the difference, it kind of sounds the same, don't it? Lissen: I remember when I was a little boy I used to hear the old men when they woke in the morning, they used to sing:

dalilamdzi	*walilamdzi*	*de'lamdzi*	*seena seena*
(the dawn	is dawning	a shadow	I come home,
			I come home)

"So the *dalilamdzi*, that means the dawn, also! The old people they would hum like that when they woke up in the morning and they said: My shadow is liable to go wandering during the night and mebbe get lost and not find me again in the morning, that's why I sing to show him where I am! . . . Well, I think you are foolish to sleep

73

here in this shack where she is liable to come back and take another look at her baskets that she made herself, and her stove, and everything, her shadow is, and it may ask your shadow to go along, and there will be no more Buckaroo Doc, and we will bury you and burn all your things, your saddle, and your book, and everything, and everybody will cry . . . well, good night, Doc!"

Wild Bill stayed there several days, waiting for Jack Folsom and the other people to come back from the Hat Creek country where they had buried "the woman who had died." He was an excellent raconteur and told me many old-time stories. There are tribes where the old-time stories and "myths" (as the anthropologists call them) are stereotyped, may even be cast in a rigid form and must be recited verbatim. But not so with the Pit Rivers! A poor story-teller gives you the barest outline, in short sentences (nearly all beginning with "and then . . ."), in a monotonous voice. But a good raconteur like Wild Bill or old Mary tells it with gestures, mimicry, imitation noises — a regular theatrical performance. If there are several people in the audience they grunt in approval after each telling passage. Instead of applauding by clapping as we do, they raise their chins and say: Hunh. . . .

Finally, one day about noon, Jack and all the relatives returned; five or six wagons full of them, and immediately everything was confusion and pandemonium in this quiet corner of the sagebrush behind the little hill. They started a big bonfire. There was a lot of argument going on. Some of the people were still wailing. A woman would come dragging things out of the house, maybe two or three baskets, maybe an armful of clothes, and throw them into the fire; then she would go out a little way into the sagebrush and wail. The men were mostly silent and preoccupied; some of them wailed in man fashion: a sort of deep grunt, Honh-ho-ho, honh-ho-ho. . . . They carried things swiftly out of the house, threw them into the fire, and went back for more. Some of them were arguing (they wouldn't have been Pit Rivers if there hadn't been some kind of argument going on!); there was a little man who kept coming to me and complaining that they ought to burn the house, also. That seemed to be a moot point because in the old days there were no individual houses. And besides, according to Wild Bill, it was Jack's house, as well as the woman's who had died. . . . But the little old man was all for destruction. At least they should throw the stove into the fire. "But it won't burn!" said Wild Bill. "Well, throw it into the creek, then," said the fundamentalist.

I was sitting in my little tent, trying to keep out of the way. All this had happened so fast, like a whirlwind out of the sagebrush, that I was dazed. But everybody kept coming into my tent either to prove to me or to themselves that they were right, or to ask me if this or that object were mine, before throwing it into the fire. My copy of *Moby-Dick* nearly went, and a horse's hackamore that belonged to me. Wild Bill stuck in my tent most of the time, sardonic as usual: "That's Indians for you! Just watch them, Doc. . . . Crazy goddam bunch. Always argue, always argue; argue all the time . . . I wish they would get through with that burning. I have three colts I am breaking, at Tuluukupi, I left them in the corrals, I guess them fellows will feed them . . . still, I ought to be getting back to them."

Jack Folsom himself didn't seem to be doing anything except going around, wailing, crying, grunting. He came into my tent and sat on my cot and sobbed like a little child. "She was very good, that woman, Doc. She never quarreled. I have had four, no, five, before her. We have been together a long time now. You know my daughter Jessie, well she raised her. Jessie has got grandchildren now."

"But, Jack, I thought Jessie was this woman's daughter. . . ."

"No, another woman's. I have had three women already, no, four. No, two only, according to Indian way. This woman I paid for her and she paid for me. That's according to Indian law. I gave Jack Wilson, you know . . . the old fellow who was singing that night, I gave him a white mare, she was awful fast, she had won several races for me, and her people gave me the right to fish on Hat Creek. . . . But you noticed that woman that's come in with them? She is ordering everything around, she is bossing everybody. . . ."

"Yes, I noticed her. Who is she?"

"She is younger sister of the woman who died, what we call *enun*, same as what you call "cousin." So, she has come to claim me."

"What do you mean, claim you?"

"It's this way, Doc: according to Indian law, *the dead people have got the say*; the relations of the dead person have got the right. If I had died, then my people, my relations, they are the ones who have the right to bring another man in my place. It don't matter he is an old man good for nothing. They say: We bought that woman, she belongs to us now; here's a man for her; she take him, or give us back our present; we gave you a horse for her; where is that horse? Now, this woman who died I married her according to Indian law. So, her people, her relations,

76

they come here with this other woman, and they say to me: You lost one, here's another, you got no claim against us."

"Well, then, it's all right, isn't it?"

"No, it ain't all right, Doc. I don't want that woman. She is all right. She is young, I know. She is clean; she is a good worker . . . but she is bossy as hell! She'll boss me . . . I am too old to be bossed!"

Afterwards I took Jack down to my little ranch in the mountains south of Monterey. We had to go fifty miles by horse-stage, then fifteen miles more by trail over the ridges. When we were on top of the highest ridge the sun was dipping into the ocean, and we stopped to eat some sandwiches and make a little coffee. But before he ate, Jack chewed a piece and spat some to the east, and to the north, and to the south, and to the west. "See, Doc, I am doing that because I am in a new country. Them people you don't see, them coyotes and foxes and all kinds of *dinihowis* and *damaagomes* that live around here, they don't know me, because I am a stranger. They might hurt me. So I am telling them: I am all right, I don't mean no harm to you people, see, I am feeding you; and you people don't hurt me neither, because I am a stranger but I want to be friends with you. That's the way to do, Doc, that's the good way."

Night overtook us, and we went down the steep trail in the dark. Jack was stumbling. "Say, Doc, you sure picked you a darn steep country for your homestead." We reached the cabin at last, and I lit a fire in the hearth. There was an old rock mortar, of the kind the Indians use to pound acorns with a stone pestle. They still use them in Central California, but, for some reason which I don't understand,

Jaime de Angulo on Chulo, March 1919

they don't use them any more in Pit River country. Indeed, the Pit River Indians are afraid to touch them. "Them things are dangerous, Doc, them things are full of power. You come across one lying on the ground, some place; and next day you'll find him mebbe a mile further away! He moved during the night!" Whether it was only the ones that were lying abandoned "some place," or whether it was *all* mortars, I never found out. Anyway, I never saw any in use among the Pit Rivers. And now, Jack was very much shocked because I had one of these mortars lying near the hearth! "You shouldn't do that, Doc! He is getting too hot there, near the fire . . . make him mad . . . he is liable to hurt you, bring you bad luck, maybe make your children sick. . . ."

But Jack did not stay very long at my little ranch. He was having bad dreams. "I been dreaming of blood, Doc. It's those people working against me, my wife's people, the one who died. They have got some powerful doctors on their side. I should have married that sister of hers when she came to claim me. That's Indian law. I can't get out of it!"

So I put him on the stage and he went back to Modoc and the joys of matrimony.

When I saw him the next summer he looked subdued. He greeted me with his usual warmth, but when I asked him how he was getting along with quondam sister-in-law, he said: "Oh, it's hell, Doc, just hell. I don't draw a free breath of my own."

I saw him again the next summer. He was radiant. "I got rid of her, Doc. I was camped at Davis Creek, and her brother he come and see me, and he says: Jack, I wouldn't stay with that woman, if I were you. She is too damn bossy! . . . Well, Doc, that's all I wanted to hear. He was her elder brother, so he had the say. So I called my own boy, Millard, you know him, and I said: I am going — when that woman comes back to the camp, don't tell her where I am gone — you don't know nothing about it, *sabe*?"

A few years later I found her married to Sukmit, of all people! But she had found her mate. They were yelling at each other, while old Mary smiled on complacently. Old Mary had earned her rest.

TWO ACHUMAWI TALES

INTRODUCTION

The Achumawi live along the course of the Pit River, in northeastern California. The following two stories were obtained from Mary Martin, an old woman of the Atwam-zini group. She herself had learned them from "Captain Jim," who was already an old chief when she was yet a young woman.

For the sake of accuracy, we give here the Indian names of the dramatis personae:

Cocoon Man is à•pónáhá. It is the caterpillar of a large moth with showy spots on its wings. The caterpillar spins itself a cocoon in the twigs of bushes and willows. He is an important personage in many myths, always appearing as a wise and sedate old chief.

These stories were collected by Jaime de Angulo and L. S. Freeland; they were first published by *The Journal of American Folk-Lore* in 1931.

His son is Woodworm. This is a fat white worm found under the bark of pine trees, especially of sugar-pines. In ordinary life it is called ámòq. His traditional name in the myths is látàùqát. He is also called the Pitch Eater, màkáh-àwámmìyé•wà, because he feeds on the sweet resin of the sugar-pine. An inoffensive and shy young man, but very handsome.

Weasel, yàs; Wolf, tsìmmù; Marten, tàmàthé; Wildcat, né•tsá•lé; Cougar, dà'tsá•lé, all of them great hunters.

Old Man Coyote, dzé•mùl, whimsical old fool. His two daughters are Eagle, lá•wí•dzá and Loon, qàmà'wìslá. Eagle is the model Indian girl: she makes baskets, cooks, and keeps quiet. Loon is the typical Indian bad girl, always flirting, always making trouble, and worst of all, careless about her menses.

Big Spider is tsàhá. Little Spider is né'né•yà.

The Giant Lizard is called kúíllàh in ordinary life. His traditional name in the myths is pílìmàìdzì. He is also called wà'wá lúnnéh, Big Lunneh. The last term has no equivalent in English; it is applied to people who are in mourning for a child. Giant Lizard had lost all his children and it made him somber and quarrelsome.

Bluejay is qàsqà•à.

Tule Bird is Tsànúnné•wà. This appears to be the traditional myth name of snipe, killdeer, or some such small bird who frequents the marshes.

Jaime de Angulo and L. S. Freeland

THE FURY OF LOON WOMAN

They all lived in Cocoon Man's winter-house. Cocoon Man was an important chief. He had a son. He kept him at the back of the house. He kept him rolled up in a white buckskin. He never took him out.

They all lived in Cocoon Man's winter-house. There was Wolf, there was Weasel, there was Marten, there was Wildcat. They all lived in there. And there was Coyote also, Coyote Old Man. He was an old chief too. He had two daughters: Eagle Girl and Loon Woman.

These two girls never slept in the house. They went outside every night. They slept in a camp of their own. Every morning they came in early and cooked breakfast. Then Eagle Girl sat near the fire and made baskets all day.

Every day the men went out hunting, all except Coyote Old Man and the Cocoon Chief. But for a long time now they had no luck. And old chief Cocoon Man said: "There is something wrong. I think it is one of these girls. I think one of them is menstruating. That's why you don't find any game. Her mother made trouble that way once long ago. I remember it all. It happened long ago."

Eagle Girl didn't say anything. She went on making her basket. Loon Woman pretended not to hear. She kept on laughing and teasing the men as usual.

That night, Wildcat stole out of the house. He went to the girls' camp. He slept with Loon. She never woke up. But in the morning, when she went out to urinate, it burnt. Then she knew somebody had been with her.

That night she smeared pitch on her belly. Then
Wildcat came, and he slept with her all night, and in the
dawn he went back to the winter-house. He was ashamed
of his belly, all black with pitch. He lifted the flap over the
smoke-hole. He let himself down the ladder. Nobody
awoke. He crawled back to his own sleeping-place. He lay
down on his belly. He crossed his arms and laid his head
on them. He went to sleep.

In the morning Loon woke up. She looked at her
belly. She saw the Wildcat's hairs. She knew. She didn't say
anything. Eagle Girl went over to the winter-house to
cook breakfast for the men. But she stayed behind. "I'll go
pretty soon," she called.

Then she went. She sat on top of the house. She threw
back the door-flap. She crouched there, looking at them
eating their breakfast. Nobody paid any attention to her.
Then she started to sing: "I want a man! I want a man! I
want a man!" But nobody paid any attention to her.

Loon laughed. Then she edged close to the smoke-
hole. She crouched there, and shot her lightning out.

Everybody jumped up, and Weasel cried: "What's the
matter with you! You will burn the house!"

Then she sang again: "I want a man! I want a man! I
want a man!"

Then her father Coyote said: "All right, I'll go with
you. We will find a man for you." — "No, I don't want to
go to find a man. I want a man who is right here." — "You
can't do that. They are all related to you here." — "I don't
care!"

Cocoon Chief said: "Better let her have her way."

Then Wolf got up. He put down his bowl of acorn
mush. He went to the foot of the ladder. He looked up:
"Do you want me?"

She sang. "Go back! Go back! I want a man! I want a man! I want a man! You are not the one!"

When she saw that all of them went back to their food, she laughed and she let out the lightning again.

Weasel jumped up. "Heee! You! Hee, up there, you! Stop it! Don't you see you will burn this house?"

"I want a man! I want a man! I want a man!" she kept on singing and laughing.

Then Fox got up and went to the foot of the ladder: "Do you want me?" — "Go back! Go back! You are not the one I want. I want a man! I want a man." Then she let the lightning out again. She strode across the smoke-hole. She let it out.

The lightning was flashing through the house. It made a great noise. Then Weasel went again to the foot of the ladder, and he cried: "Stop that! Stop that! You will burn everybody! Whom do you want? — "I want a man! I want a man! I want a man!" she sang.

They talked it over among themselves. Old Man Coyote was not in it. He was rolling string at the back of the house. Loon was his daughter. Old Cocoon Man was watching Old Man Coyote.

They decided to try Marten. He went to the foot of the ladder. He called: "Do you want me for a husband?" — "Go back! Go back! I want a man! I want a man! I want a man!"

They were all talking now. Then she let out the lightning again. Weasel jumped up: "Stop it! Stop it, I tell you! Who do you want? Do you want that fellow there?" He was pointing to Wildcat who had been sleeping all along, with his face buried in his arms.

Then they all started after Wildcat. They threw down their baskets of mush. They pounced on Wildcat. They rolled him over. Then they roared with laughter while he tried to hide his belly. They shoved him to the foot of the ladder. "Here is your husband! Here he is! Take him! Take him away and leave us alone!"

Tshllkk! Tshllkk! Tshsilllihhhhh!. . .She let it out again. Then she sang: "Go back! Go back! I want a man! I want a man!"

Then Loon jumped in through the smoke-hole and came running down the ladder. She ran to the wall. She pulled him out, the Woodworm in his bundle. The old chief Cocoon Man jumped in between. He pulled her back by the shoulder. He said: "You can't do that!" — "But I want him for my lover!" — "You can't have him!" — "But I want him."

She had the buckskin bundle in the middle of the floor. Old Chief Cocoon snatched it back and rolled it against the wall.

She got it out again. He pushed it back. She grabbed it again. He cried: "This is my son, you can't have him." They were rolling around the floor of the winter-house. She let the lightning out again. The people said to the chief: "Let her have him before she destroys us. Can't you see she is crazy?" — "But he is my son!" — "We can't help it. Everybody is going to be destroyed."

Then the old chief gave it up. She unrolled the bundle. Everybody was looking on. She unrolled him. He was all white. He was the Woodworm, some call him the Pitch Eater. "That's the one I want," she cried.

He stood up and blinked his eyes. Nobody said anything. She looked back at him. She started up the ladder. Nobody said anything. He followed after her.

Weasel said: "He'll never do! Look at him! That little thing!. . .Can't do it! Not her!. . .She'll be back with

86

her lightning and burn us all! She is crazy! Why, he is not bigger than a raddish!"

Then they all stripped off their members and gave them to the Woodworm.

Now he had a great big one. He hauled it with both hands, but it still dragged on the ground. He tripped on it. Everybody laughed. Loon Woman was out on the roof waiting.

The Pitch Eater went up the ladder after his wife. Everybody jeered. But Old Man Coyote was standing under the ladder. He was pitying his daughter. "Not that thing! It's too big! It's much too big! Can't stand it! Burst her all apart!" And as the Pitch Eater went up the ladder, he yanked it off. He threw it in the fire. Nobody knew it.

Now they were traveling along. The Loon Woman, then her lover behind her, all ashamed. Loon Woman was hot with desire. Her lover hung back. "Hurry up," she cried, "look at the storm coming!" And, out of her own thinking she made clouds come. He hurried after her.

She was making a bed for them. She laid a lot of pine needles first. Then she laid moss. She made a good bed for them, while he looked on.

Then he lay down on his belly, and he put his head on his folded arms, and he spread his legs apart, to brace himself.

She was on top of him. She tried to turn him over. She tried everything. She tried all night.

At daybreak, she fell asleep, exhausted.

Then he slid from under her. He went around in the forest. He found a stump. "That one with the arm sticking out will do," he said. He stuck hair over it, like wildcat's.

He dragged it back. She was still sleeping. He shoved it into her. She said: "Ooooh! my darling." Then he started to run back toward the winter-house.

He arrived there breathless. He couldn't speak. Weasel ran up the ladder to the top. Pitch Eater was trying to tell them about it, but Weasel's cry rang out: "There she comes with the fire! Didn't I tell you? There she comes. She is way off yet, but she is coming!"

Then they cried, "What shall we do? She is coming with the fire!" — "Oh, don't lose your head! We can manage her!" — "No, we can't do anything!" — "Surely we can!" — "But look, there she is coming with the fire!"

She was coming with the fire across the plain.

Then they sent for the Spider Brothers. Then they sent for the one who had lost his children, the Giant Lizard. He was always mourning for his children. He was the best bow-man of them all.

Big Spider made a thread. Then the One-Without-Children tied an arrow to it. He drew back. He took aim into the sky. He let go! The arrow came back. "The string isn't long enough!" he said.

They called in Little Spider "Can't you and he splice your threads together?"

Then Little Spider spun out his thread. They spliced it with the thread of his brother. And the Giant Lizard, the Big-One-Who-Had-Lost-His-Children, tied it again to the end of his arrow. He braced himself under the smoke-hole. He drew back. He shot into the sky. The arrow went up. The rope was hanging from the sky.

Weasel cried: "Hurry up! She is getting near!"

Then they told Coyote Old Man to go up first. But he did not want to do it. "I am an old man. I can't go up that way!" They tried to bully him into it. He wouldn't go.

Weasel cried down: "Hurry up! Hurry up! She is almost near!"

Then they started up, climbing the rope. Eagle Girl went first. Behind her came the Cocoon Chief. After him came his son, the Pitch-Eater Worm. Then came another one. After him came the Lizard. After him came all the rest. The last one was Coyote Old Man.

He came behind the others, crying and crying: "Oh, my daughter! Oh, my daughter!"

They said to him: "Don't look back! You mustn't look down! Don't look down! Come along with us!"

They were going up and up towards the sky. Down below the winter-house was burning. When Loon got there, she found nobody. She burnt the house. She danced in a fury. Then she saw the rope hanging from the sky. She looked up. She saw them climbing, almost up to the sky. She cried: "My father! My father!"

Coyote groaned, "Oh, my daughter! my daughter!"

They warned him again: "Don't pay any attention! Don't look down! You musn't look down! We are almost there."

"My father! My father! Look at me! Don't go away!"

"Oh, my daughter! my daughter!"

"Don't look down! Don't look down! We are almost there!"

Four of them were already in the sky, Eagle Girl, Cocoon Chief and his son. And the next man. The Big Lizard, the One-Who-Had-Lost-His-Children was almost there. He was reaching over to pull himself into the sky when Coyote looked down. The rope broke. They all fell down. They fell down into the fire.

Loon Woman was ready for them. She had a winnowing-basket. Coyote Old Man came down first. She caught him in her basket and threw him aside out of the fire.

She let the others fall into the fire. They were burnt.

89

She waited for their hearts to pop out. The first heart popped out. She caught it in her basket. Another heart popped out. She caught it in her basket. Another heart popped out. She caught it in her basket. She caught all the hearts in her basket.

Then she sat down and she counted them. She missed four of them. She knew they had reached the sky. But there was one more. That was Lizard's heart. She waited for it. Finally it popped out of the ashes. She tried to catch it, but it went right through her basket. It landed on top of Mount Shasta.

Loon cried because she had lost Lizard's heart. She said: "That one will be my ruin!"

Then she sat down again and threaded all the hearts. She made a collar of them. They were her beads. That was her necklace.

Then she went to look for her father, Coyote Old Man. She said to him: "Now I have to go! I have spoiled it. I will never be a real person again. I will be Loon. You will never be a real person any more. You will be Coyote. I will fly over the lakes. You must watch for me. I will be in four places. Sometimes I will be in Tule Lake. Sometimes I will be in Honey Lake. Then again I may be in Goose Lake. Or I may be in Upper Lake. Wherever I am, I'll let you know. I'll come out and cry. At dusk and at dawn, answer me. Come out of the brush at dusk and at dawn and answer me. I will know that you are still living, and you will know that I am still living. We cannot be real people any more." Then she flew off.

Bluejay lived not far from there. He was married to Tule Bird. Bluejay was a good hunter, but he had had no luck for a long time. He knew something was wrong. He said to his wife, "I think there has been trouble over there.

I think those people are dead. I think Loon Woman did it! Her mother did the same thing once before."

The next morning Bluejay went out hunting. He went in the direction of Mount Shasta. He was hunting around. Then he heard a song. He heard a beautiful song. He tried to find where it came from. He went searching all around. It was a very beautiful song. He couldn't find it. He went home. He told his wife about it.

He went hunting again the next morning. He went in the direction of Mount Shasta. He heard the same song. It was a very beautiful song. He couldn't find it. He went home and told his wife, "Tomorrow I'll go to the top of the mountain if I have to!" — "You had better leave it alone!" she said.

The next morning he went out. He climbed to the top of Mount Shasta. He heard the song. He went to a little mound. The beautiful song came from there. He scraped some dirt away. The song came out clearer. He scraped some more dirt away, carefully.

There he found him, a little bit of a thing, just so tiny, singing his song.

He was the Lizard's heart. He was the One-Who-Had-Lost-His-Children. A little bit of a thing, singing his song.

Bluejay gathered him up. He wrapped him in some moss. He put him down in his quiver. He went down the mountainside. He took him home to his wife. She cried with pity. She put him in a basket of water. She laid it by the fire, to keep warm all night.

In the morning it was a tiny little baby.

They nursed him along. It grew bigger every day. Now it was a little boy, playing around the place. Bluejay made him a bow and arrows. The little boy went around

91

shooting. He had a big forehead. It stood out like a bump. He was shooting around all the time. He liked to shoot straight up into the sky. His foster-mother had told him to. One day he shot off his own forehead.

He brought the forehead home to his foster-mother. She put it in a basket of water. She set the basket by the fire to keep it warm. In the morning it was a baby.

They nursed it. Both boys grew and played together.

Bluejay was still thinking about those people who had all been burnt. "Loon Woman must have done it!" he kept on saying; "Her mother did just the same thing!"

Bluejay's wife was Tule Bird, and she had relatives living on the edge of the lake. They had their house in the tules. Bluejay told his wife to ask her people about it. "Yes, we have seen something in the water, but we are afraid of it. It swims under the water, and it has a necklace of large beads. Old Loon Woman has something to do with it. We think so. That's the old woman's house down there, in the tules. We never go near there. We are afraid of her."

His wife told Bluejay what her people had said. In the morning he sent the Forehead Boy. He said to him: "Go over there and tell that old woman Loon that you want to borrow a boat from her. Tell her that you will give her half your fishing for it. Watch carefully, and look into the water. There is something there!"

The Forehead Boy came back in the evening. "Yes, I saw it!" he said, "It was swimming under the water. It had a necklace of hearts. It came out of the water and went into the old woman's house. It stayed there a long time. The old woman was combing her hair for her. Then there was a noise and she ran back into the water. It's a beautiful girl."

The Bluejay said: "You had better take my bow and arrows. Take good aim. Don't miss her!"

The next day the Forehead Boy borrowed the old woman Loon's boat again. "Old Woman, you are too old to fish. I am young. I am a good fisherman, but I have no boat. Lend me your boat and I will give you half my catch."

"All right!" she said, "but don't stay out so long!"

He went out into the middle of the lake. He kept looking into the water. He saw the Young Loon swimming under the water with her necklace of hearts. He shot her. He pulled her into the boat. He went on fishing. He shot a lot of ducks. He piled them on top of the Loon. He went back to the shore. "I got you a lot of ducks! I am tired and hungry!" he cried to the old woman. She said: "Go into the house and eat. I cooked supper for you!" He went into the house, while she started to unload the ducks.

Then he ran out of the house. But he left his voice behind him, singing in the house. The old woman Loon smelled blood. She threw all the ducks out of the boat. The Forehead Boy was running toward his home. His voice was still singing in the house. The old woman was throwing out the ducks faster and faster. Then she came to the body of her daughter. Then she cried.

Then she ran to the house, but there was nobody there. Then she started after him. He was running toward his home, with the necklace of hearts. She was running after him. She let out her lightning. All the brush was burning along with her as she ran.

Bluejay was watching. He made a strong wind to come by his thinking. The wind fanned back the fire. But the old Loon was still coming. She had almost caught up with the Forehead Boy. Then his brother, the Lizard, the One-Who-Had-Lost-His-Children, stood out from the brush and shot. He shot her dead.

THE MADNESS OF TSISNÁM

Marten and Weasel lived together. They were great hunters, but for a long time they had no luck in hunting. They didn't know what was the matter.

Wildcat people lived not far from there. They were having a puberty dance for Wildcat Girl. And Wildcat Girl had a bad dream about Marten.

Marten knew it. He cried: "That's what spoiled my hunting luck!" On the last day of the dance, at evening, while they were getting everything ready to sing and dance, Marten sneaked his way into the girl's menstrual hut.

Old Man Wildcat said to his wife: "Go and get that girl! It's time to start dancing."

She came back. She said: "She is gone. I can't find her." Everybody started searching for her. They looked everywhere. Her younger brother was searching for her. They searched for a month. They searched everywhere. Then they gave it up. They came back and smeared pitch on their faces and cried. But her younger brother did not come back. He kept on searching for her. He was crying all the time. Then he went crazy.

That's when he became Tsisnám. His teeth grew long like tusks. His beard grew long. He wanted to devour people. He stuck two feathers on either side of his head and he danced. Then he started home. He got to his people's place. There was a little child playing outside. He pounced on him and devoured him. Then he danced and shook the long feathers on either side of his head. He started to chase the children.

Somebody cried: "Water is the only thing he is afraid of." They threw water in his face. He ran off. But he came back. He lay in wait outside. He killed people and ate them. Then he danced.

His people didn't know what to do. Finally they left their home. They went to Tule Lake. They went to live on the island in the middle of the lake.

Marten had taken Wildcat Girl to his house. He put her to sleep under a rabbit-skin blanket. In the morning she peered through the strands of the blanket. She wondered where she was.

Marten went out. He gathered a lot of pine needles. He cooked them. Then he washed the girl with them from head to foot. Weasel sat watching. He didn't know what it was all about. "Where did you get that girl?" Marten paid no attention to him. He gave her some buckskin for clothes. Then he told her to stay there while he and Weasel went out hunting. Before he started he hung his porcupine-tail comb from a rafter. He said to her: "When it falls down you will know that I am dead."

He went out and killed a deer. Another man had been stalking that deer. It was Lizard, the Terrible One, the One-Who-Had-Lost-His-Children. He was a powerful man. When Marten shot the deer, Lizard cried: "There he goes stealing my game. I'll get even with you!" And he stepped out of the brush.

"That's a big buck you've got there. How about roasting him? Let's divide him."

Marten was scared. "That's all right! You can have all of him."

Lizard skinned the deer. Then he roasted him. While he was eating the meat, he kept digging out a hole, and every little while he took a look at Marten.

Marten knew that Lizard was going to challenge him. So he went a little way off into the bush and called his medicine. He changed his legs and arms into mahogany roots and manzanita roots. He twisted a long string of sinew. He tied one end to his belt and the other end to Mount Shasta. Then went back to Lizard.

Lizard had eaten all the deer. He got up and challenged Marten to a wrestling match. He wanted to throw him into the hole he had dug, but every time he lifted him high in the air the sinew cord twanged taut. But the last time Lizard took a mighty heave and the cord broke. He threw Marten into the pit and covered him with burning wood. But the mahogany and manzanita arms and legs were green and did not burn well. Lizard took him out half-cooked. He carried him in one hand and started for Marten's house.

When they saw the porcupine-tail comb fall from the rafter, Weasel and Wildcat Girl knew that Marten was dead. She guessed Lizard was coming. She gave Weasel a knife and told him to stand behind the center post. She herself took her place at the foot of the ladder.

Lizard arrived. He threw the half-cooked Marten down through the smoke-hole. Then he tried to break down the house by jumping on the roof. But he couldn't do it. Then he went down into the house.

Wildcat Girl was waiting for him. She embraced him and held him pinned against the center post while Weasel cut his ham-strings. He slumped to the floor. Weasel then hacked off one leg and threw it down. It made a great noise: "Pum!" Lizard's people way off heard it and they knew something had happened.

Weasel hacked off the other leg and threw it down.

"Pum!"

He hacked off an arm, and threw it down. "Pum!"

He hacked off the other arm. "Pum!"

Then Lizard's people started out to avenge their brother.

Tsisnám was living in the deserted winter-house of his people. He was feeding on fleas. He caught them and strung them on pine needles. He was singing like a child. "Lelu, lelu, lelu, lelu . . ." Then he stripped them into his mouth and chewed them with a smacking of the lips: "tshu-tshu-tshu-tshu-tshu . . ." When he heard the first "Pum!" he paid no attention. He paid no attention to the second "Pum!" The last "Pum!" was so loud that it made him jump. He ran out of the house. He smelled the air, sniffing for people. He was hungry for people to eat.

The Lizard people were on their way to avenge their brother. But Wildcat Girl was ready for them. She was heavy with child. So Weasel helped her squeeze out the baby. She suckled him and put him aside. Then she told Weasel to run away. She could shift for herself.

She hid under some trash. The Lizards came. They couldn't find her but they wrecked the house.

Wildcat Girl had changed herself into a bird. She flew out under the wreck of the house with her baby. The Lizards ran after her. . . . She lit far off and suckled her child. When the Lizards were near, she changed herself into a thistle and the wind carried her toward her old home. Then she changed back into Wildcat Girl. She ran toward the smokehole of the house. The Lizards were running behind her and getting close. She met Tsisnám coming out. She cried to him: "run for your life, they are coming after me!" He laughed and repeated: "Run for your life, they are coming after me!" She rushed down into the house. Tsisnám met the first Lizard and ate him. The other Lizards cried: "Tsisnám! Tsisnám! It's Tsisnám! Save yourselves!" They ran in all directions. Tsisnám was after them. He caught them all. He devoured them all. Then he went back to the house.

His sister had gathered all the baskets she could find. She soaked them tight and filled them with water. Then she gathered firewood and she sat with her child with the baskets of water all around her. Tsisnám came down into the house. She cried to him: "I am your sister! Don't you know me?" He answered: "I am your sister! Don't you know me?" She cried: "I am the one that you cried so much about, and you went crazy because of it. Don't you know me?" But he only repeated her words. Then he tried to grab her. She threw water in his face. He jumped back and sat against the wall, glowering. She suckled her baby. He said, "I want to eat that child!" "No, you mus'n't do that. That's your own nephew. I am your sister. Don't you know me? I am the one that Marten took away. You cried so much for me that you went crazy!" Then Tsisnám looked at her very hard and he almost remembered. Then he tried to grab the child again. She threw water in his face. He jumped back, and sat against the wall.

The firewood was getting low. She told him to go out and kill some more Lizards. While he was hunting for them she gathered some firewood quickly. Then he came back into the house and tried once more to grab the baby. All night long she had to keep him off by throwing water in his face. In the morning she made up her mind that she would have to get rid of him. She must get help from her people.

She had to leave the baby in his care. But she put it in a basket of water.

She went to her people where they lived on the island in the middle of the lake. She asked them to lend her a boat and be ready themselves. They suspected a trap. But at last she convinced them.

While she was gone Tsisnám sat watching the baby. He was hungry for it. He commenced to lick its toes. Then he started to chew one foot. The baby kicked and splattered water in his face. Tsisnám jumped back. Several times he tried to eat his nephew.

When his sister got back she scolded him. She said: "Why don't you go to the island. You will find plenty of people there to eat. I have a boat. I can take you there." He suspected a trap. But at last he consented.

She took a very large basket. She bade him hide in it. Then she started to sew on the lid. He wanted his head to stick out. She said: "No, they might see you!" Then he wanted his feathers to stick out. But she refused. At least his whiskers. But she refused again firmly. She sewed on the lid and she started to paddle the boat. She signalled to her people on the island to start from their side.

"Are we there yet?" he asked from inside the basket.

"Not yet, but very soon."

Her people met her halfway. They had plenty of rocks in their boats.

"Are we there now?"

"Almost."

Then she pushed the basket into the water. "You will never eat people any more!" They piled rocks on top of him. From down under the water they heard him repeat her words: "You will never eat people any more!"

All the people went back to their old home. She asked them to give a feast. She was looking for Weasel. They sent out invitations all around. Lots and lots of people came. She recognized Weasel among them.

She went with Weasel to the other house, and there they dug out the remains of the half-cooked Marten. Weasel took a branch of sage-brush and whipped him with it. Marten came back to life.

Tsisnám was singing at the bottom of the lake. He pulled out the feathers from the sides of his head. He pulled out his teeth. He pulled out his beard. Then he got out of the basket and swam to the shore. Now he was a human being again.

His sister saw him. She said: "Now I had better go and find my baby, if my brother has not already eaten him." Tsisnám said nothing. He hung his head in shame.

AFTERWORD

by Gui de Angulo

Jaime de Angulo was born in Paris in 1887 of wealthy Spanish expatriate parents. It seems that even as a child he was rebellious and difficult, and after his mother died, when he was fourteen, his father put him in a Jesuit boarding school. Jaime never forgave this, and it cemented his hatred for Catholicism, and for the dead society in which he was raised, and in which he felt he had no prospects. By the time he was eighteen he had decided to come to the United States.

He arrived in Colorado in the spring of 1905 and got a job as a cowboy on a cattle ranch. At first he was deliriously happy and proud, but soon lack of sleep and homesickness took their toll, and he decided to try South

America. He took a ship from San Francisco to Tierra del Fuego, but on board he was seduced into joining in a silver-mining scheme in Honduras. The mining venture never turned out, and Jaime was stranded without funds in Tegucigalpa for eight months. He got a job as a foreman of a road gang, and wrote home fascinating letters about conditions in Honduras, and about the Indians.

The next spring Jaime received money from home, and left for San Francisco, where he arrived the day of the 1906 earthquake. He helped fight the fire, and worked a few more odd jobs, and then decided that he wanted to study for a profession. With no particular interest in it he chose medicine and entered Cooper Union Medical School, transferring to Johns Hopkins in 1908.

At Johns Hopkins Jaime met his first wife, Cary Fink, the daughter of a well-off and cultured Kentucky family, and one of the school's first women medical students. Through her Jaime was introduced to socialism, feminism, and other "advanced" ideas. They were married in 1910.

But Jaime still loved the wild country; during the last year in medical school he commuted from a camp in the mountains. After graduating he took a job at Stanford — at that time a country town — doing research in genetics. He rode to work on his horse. At the end of the year, disillusioned with science, he abandoned his six years of medical training and, using up the last of his inheritance, bought into a cattle ranch in Alturas, California. It was there that he first came into contact with the Achumawi, or Pit River, Indians. They are mentioned only briefly in his letters at the time, but eight years later, when he went on his first field trip, it was the Achumawi that he chose. Of all the tribes he worked with in later years, he cared most for and felt closest to the Achumawi.

The cattle ranch failed, and Jaime returned to Carmel, where Cary was living. At that point he learned of a ranch in Big Sur, which he homesteaded during the next years, and called Los Pesares, the Troubles. During that summer, 1915, Jaime met Lucy Freeland (always called Nancy), a Vassar graduate, who was running a boarding house in Carmel with her sister Helen. Nancy became a sort of protegée of Jaime's, and he taught her many of the things that had come to interest him: Chinese calligraphy, astronomy, and entomology. He also told her about anthropology, a subject that had interested him since about 1912, and influenced her to go that fall to the University of California to study it.

In the spring of 1917 the United States entered the first World War, and Jaime joined the Army Medical Corps; that summer he was in the East connected with a program for the psychiatric testing of student pilots. For this project he was sent to Ann Arbor, Michigan, to take a course in psychiatry; his army papers were lost, and he couldn't be reassigned, so he stayed on, finally teaching the course himself. He was still there when the war ended.

In December of 1918 he returned to Carmel, and to Cary and their year-old daughter Ximena. That Christmas Nancy was in Carmel, as were Alfred Kroeber, head of the Department of Anthropology at the University of California, and Paul Radin, an instructor. Jaime met both men through Nancy, who was their student. Kroeber was to be very important to Jaime during the next years, and Radin was to be a life-long friend. Kroeber was sufficiently interested in Jaime's ideas on psychiatry and primitive thought to have him give a lecture at the University of California that spring as part of a seminar series in those subjects that Kroeber was teaching. Kroeber himself was a lay analyst.

After his lecture Jaime had the chance of studying Pomo with William Benson, a Lake County Indian, who was working on campus as an informant. Jaime wrote Cary that Benson was as interested in linguistics as he was, and that he was trying to teach Benson to write Pomo. Jaime was by then already in correspondence with Edward Sapir, whose book, *Language*, had just been published. Always fascinated by language, Jaime considered Sapir to be the greatest thinker in the field. Their correspondence continued for some fifteen years, and Sapir did a great deal to forward Jaime's career.

That summer Jaime was back again at the University of California at Kroeber's invitation, giving two summer courses: The Mental Functions in Primitive Culture and The Relation of Psychiatry to Anthropology.

The next two years were hard ones for Jaime. His marriage to Cary, which had been disintegrating for several years, ended in the fall of 1921 when Cary left, taking Ximena, to work in Switzerland with Carl Jung. Cary divorced Jaime at the end of the year, but they remained good friends for many years longer, and corresponded at length, especially about Jungianism.

That fall Jaime went on his first linguistic field trip, the trip he describes in *Indians in Overalls*, to the Achumawi in Modoc County, California. In *Indians in Overalls*, he describes going back to Pit River country several years running, but I think this is a literary device. There is no way he could have gone there before 1921, and no way he could have gone back until 1925. There are simply no blank places in the logs and correspondence he left behind. There is no record in his letters of the visit of Sukmit and his mother to Berkeley, but he wrote of

Jack Folsom's visit to the ranch, which took place in the middle of February, 1922, only a few months after Jaime's first visit to Modoc County. Jack was there a few weeks, doing linguistics with Jaime and doing a little work around the place.

That winter was a difficult one for Jaime. He missed his daughter, he was running out of money, and the weather was extremely severe. That was the winter he wrote his first novella, *Don Bartolomeo*, a dark and tragic tale of incest and damnation, which was published a year or so later. By the spring of 1922 he was in desperation and wrote everyone he knew in the world of anthropology and linguistics, looking for a job. Through the recommendations of Kroeber and Sapir he was hired by the Mexican government to take down Indian languages in southern Mexico. He was there until the spring of 1923, when he left for Zurich to visit Cary and Ximena. (Kroeber never forgave him for leaving the Mexican job.)

Jaime went to New York to get his boat to Europe, and there he met Nancy, who was in the East on business. They decided to marry, and Nancy went to Zurich with Jaime, where they both worked for some time with Jung. From Zurich they went to see Spain, and to visit North Africa; then Nancy, who was pregnant, left for home. Jaime went to see his father in the south of France, the last time they were ever to see each other.

During the next winter Jaime was in Berkeley rebuilding Nancy's house, which had been destroyed by the 1923 Berkeley fire, and during that winter he met Mabel Luhan and her Taos Indian husband Tony, who were staying in Mill Valley. Mabel was much interested in the Jungian ideas that Jaime was so enthusiastic about, and after she returned to Taos she invited Jaime to come there and

105

meet D. H. Lawrence, whom she seems to have hoped to indoctrinate in Jungianism as well. Jaime and Lawrence did not impress each other, and Mabel wrote an extremely amusing account of their meeting in her book *Lorenzo in Taos*. That summer Jaime returned to Taos with Nancy and their baby boy, Alvar, and took down the Taos language.*

Jaime's next visit to the Pit River country was in 1925, when he went, with Nancy and the baby, to visit first the Lower Lake Miwok, on whose language Nancy had been writing her dissertation, and then to the Achumawi country. Jung, who was interested in Jaime's ideas on primitive thought, seems to have been funding him at this time. This field trip was cut short but Jaime returned to the Achumawi in 1926, and that winter Jack Folsom stayed in Berkeley quite a while working with him. By that time the house on the hill had become a well-known meeting place for a wide assortment of people: anthropologists and linguists, Berkeley professors and students, and members of the young "lost generation" of the Depression years. The Sunday afternoon open-house parties were sometimes serious discussions of anthropology, sometimes wild parties to which the neighbors occasionally sent the police. (Kroeber remained hostile to the end, and warned students to stay away from the Angulos', a socially undesirable place.)

Jaime received professional recognition in 1927 when he was hired by the Committee on Research in Native American Languages, headed by Franz Boas, to do work in the languages of Northern California; over the next five years Jaime did a large part of the work funded by the

*(This period is documented in *Jaime in Taos: The Taos Papers of Jaime de Angulo*. City Lights Books)

106

Committee. In the fall of 1927 he became friends with Boas, who was teaching at Mills College, in Oakland.

During the late twenties Jaime wrote another novel, *The Reata*, later renamed *The Lariat*, and he began some stories for his children, called *Indian Tales for a Little Boy and Girl*. He also began writing some poetry.

In 1933 Jaime decided he wanted a better place to live at the ranch, which had become simply a camping place for weekend trips, and he began work on the "stone house," actually made of cast concrete.

In that summer Nancy joined him with the children, and there took place a terrible automobile accident in which Jaime was badly hurt and Alvar was killed. In shock and grief Jaime and Nancy decided to stay in seclusion at the ranch, and Jaime's career as a field worker came to an end.

In the winter of 1936 Jaime and Nancy went to live in North Beach, in San Francisco, where they worked on the Cantonese dialect of Chinese, a project that continued several years. After moving back and forth between the city and the ranch, Jaime tried to start a dude ranch at Los Pesares in 1938, and was involved in "the last cattle rustling in California," an episode that made the papers even in Europe.

Jaime wrote *Indians in Overalls* in 1942 after returning to Berkeley, although he must have rewritten it when he sent it to Blaise Cendrars in 1949. It's not clear how he got in correspondence with Cendrars, whom he never met. At this time he began what he considered his major opus, *What is Language?*, never published.

Jaime and Nancy were divorced in 1943, and he went to live in San Francisco, in the "compound," a group of little cottages and apartments that housed a bohemian group. He supported himself by giving lessons in language and mathematics to people of all ages, and by working as a janitor in the office of O.W.I.

Jaime returned to the ranch in 1945, where he was the focus of visits by old and new friends, becoming in time a legendary figure in what had become a bohemian center with the arrival of people like Harry Partch, Jean Varda, and Henry Miller — who described Jaime, rather dramatically, in his *Devil in Paradise*. (Jaime was *not* the "devil.")

In 1948, Jaime learned he had cancer, and went to the Veterans' Hospital in San Francisco for treatment. There, at the suggestion of a friend, he wrote Ezra Pound, who was in St. Elizabeth's Hospital. Pound wrote back, and their correspondence continued until Jaime's death. In the spring of 1949 Jaime, who was out of the hospital, went to Berkeley to see Nancy, who gave him back his old room in her house. For the next year he was involved in giving the stories in *Indian Tales for a Little Boy and Girl*, much expanded and rewritten, over radio station KPFA in Berkeley. He sent a manuscript of these broadcasts to Dorothy and Ezra Pound, and they were published by Hill and Wang in 1953. During the last years, Jaime had written a great deal of poetry, some of which was included in the book. Through the Pounds, *Indians in Overalls* was published in the fall issue of *The Hudson Review* in 1950.

Jaime de Angulo died in October of that year.